FIVE SCROLLS FOR ALL TIMES

Song of Songs, Ruth, Lamentations, Ecclesiastes, and Esther

A 10-WEEK STUDY WITH

Dr. Tony W. Cartledge

THE *Nurturing* FAITH™

BIBLE STUDY SERIES

© 2017
Published in the United States by Nurturing Faith Inc., Macon GA,
www.nurturingfaith.net.

Library of Congress Cataloging-in-Publication Data is available.

ISBN 978-1-63528-021-0

*Unless otherwise indicated, scripture quotations are taken from
the New Revised Version of the Bible.*

Abbreviations

ESV   English Standard Version

KJV   King James Version

HCSB   Holman Christian Standard Bible

NET   New English Translation (also known as the NETBible)

LXX   Septuagint, an early Greek translation of the Old Testament

MT   Masoretic Text, the "standard" Hebrew text of the Old Testament

NASB   New American Standard Bible, 1977 edition

NAS95   New American Standard Bible, 1995 edition

NIV   New International Version, 1984 edition

NIV11   New International Version, 2011 edition

NRSV   New Revised Standard Version

Cover photo by Tony W. Cartledge
*Temple Mount, as seen from the Dominus Flevit Church on the Mount of Olives,
and once the site of Jewish festivals associated with the Five Scrolls.*
Interior and cover design by Amy C. Cook

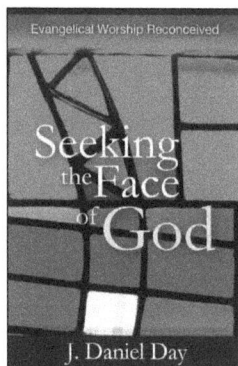
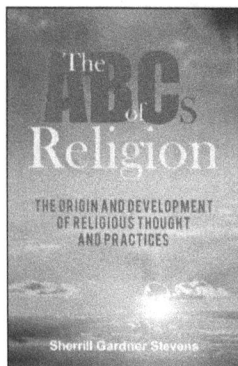

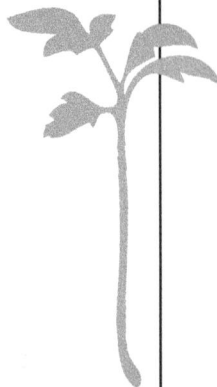

CONTENTS

PREFACE..vii

INTRODUCTION...1

SONG OF SONGS: SEX, LOVE, AND PARCHMENT SCROLLS...................7
A Woman Who Loves (Song 2:1-17)..9
A Love as Fierce as Death (Song 8:6-8)..19

RUTH: LOVE WITH A TWIST...29
"You're All I Have" (Ruth 1:1–2:23)...31
An Odd Road to a Happy Ending (Ruth 3:1–4:21).................................41

LAMENTATIONS: GOOD GRIEF..53
Sorrow Without Surrender (Lam. 1:1-22)..55
A Different Kind of Hoping (Lam. 3:1-33)...65

ECCLESIASTES: IS THAT ALL THERE IS?..73
It's Always Time (Eccl. 3:1-15)...75
Seize the Day—Every Day (Eccl. 1:2, 12-14; 2:18-23; 9:7-10)..............83

ESTHER: A NEW HOPE..91
A Tale of Two Heroines (Est. 1:1–2:18)...93
A Winning Woman (Est. 7:1-6, 9-10; 9:20-22).....................................101

AFTERWORD..111

This volume in the Nurturing Faith Bible Study Series is made possible through a generous gift from Lynda and Dan Bryson, in honor of Dan's parents, Loretta and Dee Bryson.

***

Nurturing Faith seeks sponsors for future volumes in this Bible study series. To inquire, please contact office@nurturingfaith.net.

PREFACE

I love digging into parts of the Bible that are underexplored. As an archaeological excavation can uncover layer upon layer of ancient civilizations hiding just beneath the earth's surface, so the trowel of careful study and exegesis can unearth layers of meaning that have long been overlooked.

So it is with the five brief biblical books we will study in this volume. The book of Ruth is familiar to many Christians as a story of love and devotion—but not for its deeper significance. Esther is a lesser known heroine whose story is more convoluted and troubling than it appears. The Song of Songs, with its frank eroticism, has frightened pious clerics into masking its message with allegory, while the dark books of Lamentations and Ecclesiastes may send readers fleeing to higher literary ground lest they become too deeply enmeshed in the hard questions of life.

Our purpose in these Bible studies is to tackle these texts as they have come to us, digging beneath surface pleasantries to discover the clever, hopeful, skeptical, sorrowful, delightful, and sometimes naked characters beneath. In doing so, we may see new things, think new thoughts, and seize the opportunity to appreciate the scriptures even more.

—John D. Pierce, Publisher
Nurturing Faith, Inc.

INTRODUCTION

Are you familiar with the term "Megillot" as it relates to biblical studies? If not, don't feel badly: you're not alone. The Megillot, or "Five Scrolls," are five short books tucked into various corners of the Old Testament in Christian Bibles. This arrangement makes the books less visible, as they blend into the background of the surrounding stories. That, along with the scrolls' sometimes distinctively sexy or theologically troubling messages, has kept them largely on the back burner when it comes to preaching or teaching the Bible in the church.

What do we mean by "Megillot"? The term is the plural form of the Hebrew word *megillah*, which means "scroll." The term was first applied to Esther, and later to the other four books in the collection: Ruth, Lamentations, Song of Songs, and Ecclesiastes.

The books are scattered through the Old Testament in Christian editions of the Bible. Ruth appears first, inserted into a large unit of text that stretches from Joshua through 2 Kings. Those books appear together as the "Former Prophets" in the Hebrew Bible.

Modern scholars refer to this unit as the "Deuteronomistic History" because the stories reflect and illustrate the theology of blessing and cursing characteristic of the book of Deuteronomy: they show how Israel's fortunes waxed and waned from the entry to the land of promise to the destruction of Jerusalem and the Babylonian exile. Translations from Hebrew, beginning with the Greek Septuagint from the third century BCE, inserted Ruth between the books of Judges and 1 Samuel because the story fits there chronologically and highlights the ancestry of King David.

Esther comes after Nehemiah in Christian Bibles as the last narrative account related to Israel's history in the post-exilic period. Ecclesiastes and the Song of Songs (also known as the Song of Solomon) follow Proverbs as the last two Wisdom books before the writing prophets begin with Isaiah. Lamentations was placed among the prophets because of a tradition that Jeremiah (whose book it follows) was the author, though it is not a book of prophecy.

The Megillot have a much stronger presence in the Hebrew Bible because they form a subunit within the larger section called the Kethubim, Hebrew for "Writings" (some writers use the term Hagiographa, from a Greek compound meaning "Holy Writings"). The modern Hebrew canon consists of the Torah (Law, also called the Pentateuch), the Nevi'im (Prophets), and the Kethubim (Writings). The Megillot appear among the writings, following the poetic books of Psalms, Proverbs, and Job, and preceding the concluding books of Daniel, Ezra-Nehemiah, and 1-2 Chronicles.

This was not always the case, however. A tradition preserved in *Bava Batra*, part of the Jewish rabbinic commentary known as the Talmud, lists the Megillot in their supposed chronological order among other books of the Writings, as follows: Ruth, Psalms, Job, Proverbs, Ecclesiastes, Song of Songs, Lamentations, Daniel, the Scroll of Esther, Ezra, and Chronicles (*Bava Batra* 14b).

The famed Leningrad and Aleppo codices manuscript, from the late 10th and early 11th centuries CE, group the scrolls together, but in what the rabbis interpreted as their chronological order: Ruth, Song of Songs, Ecclesiastes, Lamentations, and Esther.

Modern critical editions of the Hebrew Bible retain this order, which has Ruth and Esther as bookends, with the hard questions of Qoheleth (Ecclesiastes) in the middle, flanked by the joyful Song of Songs and the mournful book of Lamentations.

A number of medieval manuscripts, however, grouped the books of the Megillot differently, organizing them to fit the order of the annual festivals with which they are associated and read. Modern Jewish translations such as the *Tanakh* follow this order: Song of Songs, Ruth, Lamentations, Ecclesiastes, and Esther. That is also the order we will follow in this book. Let's take a quick look at a possible rationale behind this ordering of the "five scrolls."

SONG OF SONGS

The Song of Songs, called the "Song of Solomon" in many Bibles, is a frank celebration of love and sexuality. It is typically read during Passover. This is probably based on a rabbinic interpretation that the Song allegorically describes a love affair between God and Israel.

Passover is said to have originated as the Israelites were being freed from Egypt and preparing to enter a covenant with Yahweh, so the Song could be thought to celebrate the "young love" of nascent Israel for the God who delivered them. Passover occurs on the 15th–22nd of the Hebrew month of Nissan, the first month of the year in the Jewish calendar. That usually coincides with late March to mid-April, in early spring. Thus, some think of Passover as the "springtime of love" between God and Israel.

Song 2:11-13 speaks of love that buds as the winter passes and spring flowers begin to bloom. In some traditions, the Song of Songs is also read in weekly ceremonies welcoming the Sabbath, metaphorically entering as a bride.

RUTH

Ruth includes a love story, but is primarily a tale of God's faithfulness to Naomi, Ruth's mother-in-law. Since Ruth and Boaz became the great-grandparents of King David, the story points toward Israel's glory days as a monarchy under David.

Ruth is read during the Feast of Weeks on the day of *Shavuot*, which celebrates the giving of the law, supposedly 49 days after the Passover. This coincides with the Christian celebration of Pentecost, in May or June. Why read Ruth at *Shavuot*?

Some think the connection may be that Ruth 1:22 mentions the beginning of the barley harvest, which occurs about that time. It may also have something to do with a traditional (but entirely unsubstantiated) belief that David was born and died on the day of *Shavuot*. It is more likely that Ruth's decision to follow Naomi and adopt Yahweh as her God was thought to reflect Israel's receiving of the Torah and covenanting with God at Sinai.

LAMENTATIONS

The book of Lamentations is exactly that: a collection of five carefully crafted laments over the destruction of Jerusalem and the beginning of the exile for the people of Judah in 587 BCE.

Appropriately, Lamentations is read on the 9th of Av on the Hebrew calendar (July or August). This commemorates a Jewish tradition that both the first and second temples were destroyed on that same month and day.

ECCLESIASTES

The book of Ecclesiastes is a painful effort to understand the meaning of human life and God's ways. Somewhat surprisingly, it is read during the eight-day festival of Sukkot, or the "Feast of Booths," a harvest festival in the fall (usually October). Why read a cynical, depressing book during a happy festival?

Some rabbis contended that Eccl. 11:2 ("Divide your means seven ways, or even eight, for you do not know what disaster may happen on earth") is a call to rejoice during the eight days of Sukkot. Since vows may have been paid during the autumn festival, the author's warning (5:3-4) not to neglect paying vows seems appropriate. Others think the shortening days of late autumn provide a fitting background for Qoheleth's dark musings.

ESTHER

The book of Esther tells the story of how the feast of Purim began, a celebration not mentioned elsewhere in the Bible. It commemorates a story about God delivering a group of Hebrews who lived in Persia during the post-exilic period.

According to the story, Esther was a Jewish girl who had to keep her identity a secret but with the help of her kinsman Mordecai she managed to charm the royal court on her way to becoming queen before courageously foiling a plot to exterminate every Jew in the empire.

Purim, which celebrates Esther's exploits, occurs on the 14th of Adar, the 12th month of the Jewish calendar, usually early March.

CURRENT PRACTICE

The practice of reading the scrolls during Jewish festivals did not occur all at once. The reading of Esther during Purim was known in the Second Temple Period, while reading Lamentations on the 9th of Av was mentioned in the Talmud. Other readings are not mentioned until the Post-Talmudic period (after 500 CE), though their order was different than what is currently practiced.

As we can see, in Jewish worship the ceremonial readings of the Megillot begin with Passover in the month of Nissan (the first month) and conclude in Adar (the last month). Thus, the books are read in their entirety at least once each year.

In contrast, the Revised Common Lectionary readings for Sundays include just two passages from Ruth and Lamentations, and only one each from Esther, Ecclesiastes, and the Song of Songs—over a three-year period. Each of those Sundays also offers three additional readings as options for proclamation, so it's rare that most participants in lectionary-based worship will hear anything more than a scant reading from the Megillot during that time.

One could argue that the current arrangement of the scrolls may serve a purpose beyond matching up (however tenuously) with the Jewish festivals. The present order may also be seen to reflect a broad overview of Israel's history.

Consider this: the Megillot begins with a love story (Song of Songs) as God and Israel become covenant partners. Although Exodus and Numbers portray the wilderness period as a time of frequent conflict between the Israelites and God, later prophets romanticized it as a memorable time of love and courtship. Jeremiah, for example, quotes Yahweh as saying "I remember the devotion of your youth, your love as a bride, how you followed me in the wilderness, in a land not sown" (Jer. 2:2).

The sequence continues with a delightful prelude to the rise of the monarchy and the rule of King David in the book of Ruth. Though David is not mentioned by name, the happy story of human trust and divine blessing culminates in the marriage of Ruth and Boaz, which produces Obed, the father of Jesse, the father of David—and presages Israel's glory days as an independent kingdom.

Neither the monarchy nor Israelite independence lasted, however. The northern kingdom of Israel fell to the Assyrians in 722 BCE, and the southern kingdom of Judah was destroyed in 587 BCE. Lamentations mourns Israel's defeat, the destruction of the temple, the loss of the homeland, and the dark period of the exile.

The book of Ecclesiastes is timeless, but in the canonical context it picks up on the troubled period in Israel's life, reflecting from a wisdom perspective the apparent futility of making sense out of life and wondering if God truly rewards the righteous.

Out of the dismal experience of exile and scattering, however, comes the story of Esther's timely rise and heroic actions that result in the Persian Jews being saved from a planned pogrom, and their ability to rise against those who would harm them. The book of Esther never mentions God, but celebrates the cleverness and solidarity of the Jews as an ethnic group. Esther did not lead the people to independence, but her story affirms the Jews' ability to survive in the diaspora, even as a mistrusted or persecuted minority with the cards stacked against them.

The Bible studies that follow reflect the order of the books in the Hebrew Bible, where they are not only collected, but also given prominence. It is my hope that a closer look at these often-ignored books will provide helpful insight and encourage readers to think about some parts of the Bible that have spent far too long in the shadows of Protestant preaching and teaching.

SONG OF SONGS

Sex, Love, and Parchment Scrolls

Song of Songs 2:1-17

A WOMAN WHO LOVES

My beloved speaks and says to me:
"Arise, my love, my fair one, and come away . . ."
—Song of Songs 2:10

Bible studies from the Song of Songs may be even scarcer than sermons based on its beautiful but mysterious poetry, but the ancients were wise enough and inspired enough to preserve it as a part of the scriptures. This may seem strange, because the Song never mentions God or Israel, has no religious themes, and is frankly, exotically, erotically focused on human intimacy and sex with no real mention of marriage—or of sin. ⚓

So, what wisdom might we find in this surprising book?

The Song of Songs is one of five short books that the Hebrew Bible refers to as the Megillot, and it is typically read during the Passover celebration. Some of the rabbis interpreted the Song of Songs as an allegory for the love relation-

---

⚓ **How did it get in?** The Song of Songs had a hard time making it into the canon. During the first century, as the rabbis were trying to tie down the loose ends and establish the limits of the Hebrew Bible once and for all, there was considerable opposition to including the Song of Songs.

But the *Mishna*, an ancient rabbinic commentary, records that the famous Rabbi Akiva said: "Heaven forbid that there should be division in Israel about the holiness of the Song of Songs, for there is not one day in the whole of eternity that equals the one in which the Song of Songs was given to Israel. For all the Writings are holy, but the Song of Songs is the holiest" (*Mishna Yadayim* 3:5).

> 🔅 **Festive readings:** Each of the five "scrolls" (Song of Songs, Ruth, Lamentations, Ecclesiastes, and Esther) is associated with a particular Jewish feast or celebration.
>
> The Song of Songs is typically read among Ashkenazic Jews (of Eastern European ancestry) on the Sabbath before the Feast of the Passover. Among some Sephardic Jews (of Spanish or Mediterranean ancestry), it is read on the eve of every Sabbath.

ship between God and Israel, and the Passover marked the beginning of the Exodus/Wilderness period, later idealized as a type of "honeymoon" between Yahweh and Israel. 🔅

The name of the book, traditionally but erroneously called the Song of Solomon, comes from its first verse, which literally reads, "The song of songs, which is to/of/by/for Solomon." This, like the superscriptions found in the psalms, was almost certainly added by an editor of the text sometime after its initial composition. Solomon is an unlikely author of the Song, though the later editor either attributed the poems to him, or thought they should be dedicated to him.

The book, largely a collection of love poems, probably came to be associated with Solomon because two of the poems speak of the male lover as a king (1:4, 12), and several verses mention Solomon, though always in the third person—as someone else talking about him (3:6-11, 8:11-12). Solomon's accomplishments were both celebrated and probably exaggerated: the author of 1 Kings claimed that Solomon wrote 1,005 songs (1 Kgs. 4:32), and that he had an unlikely harem of 700 wives and 300 concubines (1 Kgs. 11:3). This would have given him quite the reputation of a lover, though not in the passionate or committed nature of the romantic couple (or couples) who must struggle to see each other in the Song of Songs.

Solomon was also known as a patron of the arts, and the book's association with the fondly remembered king undoubtedly added a sense of authority and helped assure its place in the canon. Even so, most modern scholars doubt seriously that Solomon had anything to do with its composition. Not only is Solomon described in the third person; much of the vocabulary reflects a period hundreds of years after Solomon ruled. While we acknowledge that some parts of the book could be very old and conceivably connected to Solomon, its final composition almost certainly belongs in the postexilic period, long after Solomon's reign, and perhaps as late as the third century. 🔅

> ♦ **Translating the Song:** Poetry is notoriously difficult to translate, and the 117 verses of the Song of Songs have more *hapax legomena* (words used only once in the Bible) than any other book in either Testament, making an accurate translation even more difficult. About 11 percent of the words in the Song do not appear elsewhere in the Bible.
>
> In many cases, we try to figure out what the words mean by comparing them to similar words in other ancient Semitic languages such as Arabic, Akkadian, Ugaritic, Sabaean, and Ethiopic. In some cases, we must admit that we don't have certain knowledge of what the words mean, requiring translators to make an educated guess.
>
> Also, quite frequently we must ask whether the writer intended for a word to be taken literally or figuratively, a factor that can affect the translation.

How did the book get its alternate name? "Song of songs" is a superlative expression, a Hebrew way of saying "the greatest song." Bibles favored by Catholics call the book "Canticles," after the title in the Latin translation known as the Vulgate.

The short book's 117 verses comprise anywhere from five to 50 different poems, depending on how one counts them. The book is not a unified, lyrical love song, nor does it portray a clear drama, though some scholars have labored to identify a cohesive plot and identify speaking parts. The book is a rather loose collection of love poems that probably refer to more than one couple. Just how the Song functioned in Israel's life and worship is unclear. ♦

A fascinating aspect of this book is that, despite the patriarchal dominance of Israel's history, the female lover plays a positive and powerful role in the Song. The woman is not a passive target for the man's affection, but appears just as bold as he in describing what she admires, what she wants, and how she plans to find time with her lover. She is assertive and sexual and clearly appreciates the joy of intimacy apart from its role in procreation or patriarchal family systems. Another interesting angle is that she often speaks of her mother's house and her mother's bedchamber, both of which speak of female power or autonomy in lovemaking.

If there is a hint at traditional stereotypes in the Song, it is that the young woman, while not uninterested in her lover's physical appearance, seems more interested in his embrace. In contrast, the male lover comes across as more visual, with more frequent descriptions of the maiden's beauty, shape, and sexy attributes. The frequency with which the woman speaks suggests the distinct possibility that a woman could have written all or part of the Song of Songs.

🜂 **Function:** Scholars have long debated how the Song functioned in Israel's life, with suggestions ranging from a fertility ritual to a funerary practice. Some see it as a collection of wedding songs, or simply a collection of popular love songs similar to those known from Egypt.

Some have sought to reconstruct the book as a drama including several speakers and a chorus made up of the daughters of Jerusalem (or brothers of the woman). Some translations include periodic headings to indicate which person the translators think is speaking. There is no consensus about how and where the material is divided into units, and who is speaking. Nor is it clear that the male lover identified as a shepherd and a king are the same man, whether they are vying for the love of the same maiden, or whether the poems are unconnected.

None of the arguments are wholly convincing. Just as it's hard to neatly define love and tie it up with a bow, we can't fit the Song into a neat package. Perhaps it is best to simply regard it as a collection of ancient love songs that celebrate young love, the discovery of love, sexual awakening, and the hopes of the lovers.

One possible reason for the popularity of these songs and their eventual collection could be that they often seem to speak of forbidden love, of love that cannot be expressed in the public square or that public officials might not approve. While there are probably multiple characters here, not just two, several of the poems speak of lovers who may seem mismatched by society's standards, but who sought to overcome the obstacles and be with their true chosen partner.

Forbidden love has remained a common theme in literature or popular music through the years: just think of *Romeo and Juliet, West Side Story*, or the movie version of *Titanic*, among others. In the postexilic period, the theme might have had special resonance for those who were caught in Ezra or Nehemiah's campaign to prevent intermarriage between "pure" Israelites and any of their ethnically mixed neighbors.

LOVE DESIRED
(2:1-9)

Our text describes an encounter involving a young woman who could have been named "Flower"—she describes herself as "a rose of Sharon, a lily of the valleys" (v. 1), while her beloved describes her as "a lily among brambles" (v. 2). She likewise describes her beau in lavish terms as a rare find, "like an apple tree among the trees of the wood" (v. 3). 🜂 "I sat in his shadow," she says, "and his fruit was sweet to my taste." The image of shade suggests both protection from the blazing sun and the delight of a secretive location. Beneath the shadow of her beloved, she

> ☙ **Apples:** Apple trees were not native to Palestine. Then, as now, the kind of apple trees that produce good fruit must be carefully cultivated, and to find such a tree "in the wood" would be an unexpected boon.
>
> Apples, though uncommon, were known throughout the ancient Near East, and often associated with themes of romantic love and sexual fertility. References to apples or apple trees occur several times in the Song: 2:3, 5, 7, 9; 8:5.

extends the metaphor with a figurative description of their happy and obviously sexual encounter.

The notion of taste continues in v. 4, where they come to "the banqueting house" (literally, "house of wine"), a metaphor for the feast of love they share. She recalls asking for raisin cakes and apples for sustenance in her love-sick state (v. 5), but the cure she most desires is to be in her beloved's arms: "O that his left hand were under my head and that his right hand embraced me" (v. 6). ☙

Enamored with thoughts of love, the maiden calls on her companions, the "daughters of Jerusalem," to swear that they will not "awaken or arouse love" until "it delights" (literally), sometimes translated "until it is ready" (v. 7, NRSV). Here, as in many other places in the Song, "love" is not abstract, but descriptive of physical passion. The meaning seems to be that one should be cautious, and not arouse one's ardor before the time is right.

Anticipating a new encounter (v. 8), the maiden exults in the sound of her beloved's voice and the sight of his approach. She describes him as being like a gazelle or a young stag (v. 9), "leaping upon the mountains, bounding over the hills." Both stags and gazelles, sure-footed residents of the area's mountain crags and open plains, were often associated with male virility in the ancient Near East.

> ☙ **His embrace:** The first part of v. 6 has no verb: "his left hand under my head" could thus be rendered in different ways. "His left hand [is] under my head," and "[O that] his left hand [were] under my head" are two options. Whether she is wishing for his embrace or describing it depends on the translator's understanding of the surrounding context, in which the verbal forms can be translated differently.
>
> The healing power of a lover's embrace is reflected in Egyptian love poetry, as in these lines: "My salvation is her coming in from outside; when I see her, I will be healthy. When she opens her eye, my body is young; when she speaks, I will be strong. When I embrace her, she exorcises evil from me" (from the Chester Beatty Papyri, C 5:1-2, cited in notes to Song 2:6 in the New English Translation).

The maiden anxiously watches for his arrival, and happily spots him standing behind the wall, peeking through the lattice—a suggestion that their tryst is a secret one.

> **For Reflection:** *Have you ever been so enamored with a new love interest that you could not wait to see him or her again? How do you distinguish between the early glow of infatuation and the deeper bond of love?*

LOVE INVITED
(2:10-15)

With v. 10, the beloved arrives, and his voice—quoted by the woman—is heard in the next several verses. The man is just as eager to see the woman as she is to be reunited with him. In words reminiscent of an ode to spring he bids her come away with him, apparently to relish their love amid the beautiful world of springtime.

With the passing of winter rains (v. 11)—when planting was done—springtime offered a window of opportunity for other pursuits. Kings led their armies to war in the spring because the troops weren't needed in the fields until harvest (2 Sam. 11:1). The same freedom brought the man to his beloved, declaring that spring had arrived and it was time for love.

As romantic partners today enjoy hiking mountain trails, strolling through floral gardens, or ambling along a beach, the man calls the woman to come away with him. He speaks of flowers, birdsong, fig trees, and fragrant vineyards—all possible background settings for secretive expressions of love (vv. 12-13).

Despite her earlier enthusiasm, the woman appears to have become fearful. The male lover speaks of her as a dove hiding in one of the many small cavities characteristic of the pockmarked rocky cliffs of Palestine (v. 14). He calls her to come out of hiding so he can see her face and hear her voice, "for your voice is sweet, and your face is lovely." ⛏

With v. 15, the woman speaks again, apparently giving voice to her fears. Whether she is speaking to her lover or to a wider audience is unclear,

> ⛏ **Chiasm**: The latter part of v. 14 offers a nice example of a chiastic parallelism, in which elements appear in reverse order: face-voice-voice-face.
>
> *Let me see your face,*
> *let me hear your voice;*
> *for your voice is sweet,*
> *and your face is lovely.*

but she appeals for someone to "catch the foxes, the little foxes that ruin the vineyards, for our vineyards are in blossom."

Earlier, the man had spoken of vineyards in blossom, and now the woman returns to the image as a metaphor for their love, which appears to be threatened. Several of the poems in the Song speak of lovers who don't match up with social conventions and are thus discouraged from meeting, leading them to meet at night or to arrange secretive outdoor trysts.

Who were the foxes that threatened the couple's love, which was just in bloom? The poem does not say, but evidence in other parts of the Song point to possible ethnic or class differences. In 1:5 she speaks of being "black but beautiful." This statement probably relates more to social class than to race, for she attributes her dark skin to being forced to work outdoors as a vine-keeper.

In chapter 5, when the woman goes out in search of her lover, she is caught and beaten by night watchmen, though the cause of her offense is not clear. Someone did not want them to be together.

> **Foxes:** Foxes are mentioned several times in the Hebrew Bible, always in a negative sense (Judg. 15:4, Neh. 4:3, Ps. 63:10, Lam. 5:18, Ezek. 13:4). With a taste for sweet grapes, they could cause significant damage to a vineyard. Thus, well-tended vineyards were surrounded by sturdy fences or hedges and included a watchtower so someone could keep an eye out for intruders (see, for example, Isa. 5:1-2).
>
> An old Jewish Midrash (an early commentary on scripture) includes a story about a fox that fasted for three days so he could squeeze through a hole in the fence to enter a vineyard. After eating his fill, however, he had to fast another three days to get back out!

LOVE ENJOYED
(2:16-17)

Whatever obstacles they had to overcome, the lovers achieve their rendezvous, and the woman describes their love (or perhaps lovemaking): "My beloved is mine and I am his," she says. Then, with a description of sex barely veiled in metaphor, she adds: "he pastures his flock among the lilies" (NRSV, or NET: "he grazes among the lilies," v. 16). The woman hopes the encounter will last through the night ("until the day breathes and the shadows flee"), urging her beloved to "be like a gazelle or a young stag on the cleft of the mountains" (v. 17).

What do we do with such a frank and erotic description of love between two people? Why is this in scripture?

❂ *'Ani ledodi*: A variation of the expression "I am my beloved's, and my beloved is mine" appears at 2:16, 6:3, and 7:10. The first line of 6:3, *'ani ledodi, vedodi li* (literally, "I belong to my beloved, and my beloved belongs to me") has become a popular phrase for incorporation into jewelry such as necklaces, bracelets, and rings.

A ring bearing the Hebrew script (right to left) for *'ani ledodi, vedodi li.*

As noted earlier, interpreters have employed a variety of approaches in trying to make sense of the text, or to make it palatable to prudish readers. While the allegorical approach may have been the most popular method, it is exegetically the least satisfying, for such an interpretation has to be imposed on a text that doesn't really invite it.

In the end, we may regard this and other texts from the Song of Songs as a welcome biblical endorsement of the wonder and beauty of love, passion, and sexual encounter as being among God's most beautiful and praiseworthy gifts.

The man considers the woman to be a "lily among the brambles" (v. 2) while she considers him to be "an apple tree among the trees of the wood" (v. 3). Both are symbols of a rare and cherished find. Surely that kind of joyful, devoted relationship has something sacred about it, something worthy of poetry and song—even of scripture.

For Reflection: *How do you think the Song of Songs should be read: as a celebration of sexual love, an allegory of spiritual love, or possibly both?*

THE HARDEST QUESTION
How do we interpret the message of the Song of Songs?

The Song of Songs, with its frequent and graphic references to sex—and its complete absence of any reference to God—has left both Jewish and Christian interpreters uncomfortable. How do we understand this elegant but racy collection of love poems?

Through the years, expositors have developed a variety of interpretational approaches. Perhaps the most popular tactic is to treat the Song as an allegory about God's love relationship with Israel or the church. That approach works better in a generic fashion than a specific one, however: it's one thing to speak of the church as the bride of Christ, but quite another to describe the relationship in a graphic, physical, sexual way.

It appears clear that the poets or writers who contributed to the Song of Songs had other things in mind when composing the alluring and erotic poetry that makes up the book. They certainly made no effort to spell out any sort of connection or allusion to the man and woman as God and Israel.

It is quite possible to recognize the book as a frank celebration of sexual love as God's good gift to humankind. The lack of specific references to God or marriage, along with the abundance of creation images, suggest that the book's main purpose may be simply to extol God's good gift of human sexuality and its expression in loving relationships—even in situations outside of typical societal bounds.

Perhaps it is best to recognize that the poetry of the Song can be read on more than one level. On the surface, the poetry speaks openly about love and sex, eroticism and intimacy, the excitement of longing for the touch of a loved one.

On a different level, the song could be read as a commentary on the theme of barriers such as race and class or religion and family that can interfere with love. Like *West Side Story* or *Romeo and Juliet*, it can be seen as a plea for understanding and acceptance for relationships between people from different backgrounds. This would have been especially apropos during the postexilic period, when religious leaders were demanding that Hebrew men and women should avoid intermarriage with non-Jews.

On a more abstract level, one could possibly read the song as an allegory of longing and love, pursuit and courtship between God and people—but one should be aware that such an interpretation is imposed from without by later tradition or current readers, and almost certainly was not the author's intent.

Song of Songs 8:6-8

A LOVE AS FIERCE AS DEATH

Set me as a seal upon your heart,
as a seal upon your arm;
for love is strong as death,
passion fierce as the grave.
—Song of Songs 8:6-8

Is anything more thrilling than romantic love, especially as expressed through sexual activity? (No need to answer aloud!). Many readers are surprised to learn that the Bible contains a book that boldly focuses on love, including its sexual expression. Some would rather not acknowledge it, and insist that the Song of Songs was designed only as an allegory of love between God and Israel, or God and the church.

Despite later references to the church as the "bride of Christ," the application of explicit sexual metaphors to the divine-human relationship seems overly forced. While the book might be read on two levels, the Song of Songs, on the face of it, is primarily about human love, the passion that lovers can have for each other, and the power of love to overcome social barriers or the disapproval of others.

Given the inherent appeal of the subject—and the church's persistent habit of overlooking its presence in scripture—a closer look at the Song of Songs can be worthwhile.

In this lesson we will consider the various types of love poetry found in the Song, then conclude with a look at three powerful verses that could be at home in every wedding ceremony.

POEMS OF DESCRIPTION

The main characters in the Song are two people who are deeply in love. Though its structure remains elusive, the book is clearly a collection of poems about love between a man and a woman who celebrate their admiration of each other in a variety of ways. While one could imagine the same two lovers throughout the book, the various settings suggest that the book may reflect situations in which different couples speak of their ardor and devotion.

⬥ **Terrible, or awesome?** Two poems employ metaphors that appear most curious at first, at least in some translations. Twice the woman is described as being "terrible as an army with banners" (6:4, 10; NRSV, KJV). The word translated as "terrible" can mean that, but is better read as "awesome," "awe-inspiring" (NET), or "majestic" (NIV11). Her beauty and presence are not "terrible" in a negative way, but as captivating as the awe-inspiring sight of an army approaching beneath impressive colored banners.

The book contains various types of poetry, including physical descriptions of the two lovers, both by each other and by other people. Several examples of the descriptive poems are similar to a *wasf*, a type of Arabic poetry that describes parts of the male or female body from the top down, or from the bottom (no pun intended) up. These may use images from plant or animal life, from architecture, or even from the military as metaphorical language to create a sensory image of the body that includes scents as well as sights. ⬥

For example, in 4:1-7, the man describes his beloved's features, beginning with her head and moving downward, probably to her pubic area. The quotation is from the NET translation:

Oh, you are beautiful, my darling! Oh, you are beautiful! Your eyes behind your veil are like doves. Your hair is like a flock of female goats descending from Mount Gilead.
Your teeth are like a flock of newly-shorn sheep coming up from the washing place; each of them has a twin, and not one of them is missing.
Your lips are like a scarlet thread; your mouth is lovely. Your forehead behind your veil is like a slice of pomegranate.
Your neck is like the tower of David built with courses of stones; one thousand shields are hung on it—all shields of valiant warriors.
Your two breasts are like two fawns, twins of the gazelle grazing among the lilies.

Until the dawn arrives and the shadows flee, I will go up to the
  mountain of myrrh, and to the hill of frankincense.
You are altogether beautiful, my darling! There is no blemish in you!

Some metaphors are more obvious than others. While the notion of hair as
goats (v. 1) may not hold initial appeal, the idea is that her long and wavy hair
moves in cascades reminiscent of sure-footed goats running down a steep moun-
tainside. Most modern people would not compare one's teeth to farm animals (v.
2), but the image of freshly washed sheep indicates not only that her teeth are
white, but also evenly matched, with none missing. The fruit of a halved pomegranate is red, so the image of v. 3 probably refers to the rosy glow of her cheeks.

The man's description of her neck as the Tower of David surrounded by
shields (v. 4) is more of a compliment than it may appear: he probably intends
to say that her neck is long and symmetrical, enhanced by necklaces reminiscent
of military shields hung around a tower. The reference here and elsewhere to the
woman's breasts as being like fawns or gazelles (v. 5) does not mean they look like
contemporary "reindeer boobs" posted on Instagram, but that they bounce. The
"mountain of myrrh" and "hill of frankincense" (v. 6) are synonymous references
to the same thing, probably her pubic mound, which he finds as perfect as the
rest of her.

While the former poem describes the woman from the top down, a depiction
in 7:1-6 (NET) begins with her feet and works upwards:

How beautiful are your sandaled feet, O nobleman's daughter!
  The curves of your thighs are like jewels, the work of the hands of a
  master craftsman.
Your navel is a round mixing bowl—may it never lack mixed wine!
  Your belly is a mound of wheat, encircled by lilies.
Your two breasts are like two fawns, twins of a gazelle.
Your neck is like a tower made of ivory. Your eyes are the pools in
  Heshbon by the gate of Bath-rabbim. Your nose is like the tower of
  Lebanon overlooking Damascus.
Your head crowns you like Mount Carmel. The locks of your hair are
  like royal tapestries—The king is held captive in its tresses!
How beautiful you are! How lovely, O love, with your delights!

In this poem, too, some metaphors require a bit of exposition, and some
remain mysterious.

The word translated as "navel" in v. 2 is a *hapax legemonenon*, meaning that it
occurs only once in the Bible. Competing evidence from cognate languages and

the design of the poem has led to considerable debate about whether it should be translated as "navel" or "vulva." Since the progress is from feet to thighs and upward, one would reach the vulva before the belly, and the moist image of wine might be more appropriate in that context.

The belly as a "mound of wheat encircled by lilies" doesn't sound flattering, but may reference the pubic mound. Images of wine and wheat (for bread) may indicate the woman's ability to satisfy his sexual hunger.

Similar images are used for her fawn-like breasts and her neck, which is long and symmetrical like a tower, as smooth as ivory.

The reference to the gate of Bath-rabbim is obscure, because the site is unknown. Mount Carmel is a majestic mountain that towers beautifully above the coastal plain. The idea that the beloved's nose is like the Tower of Lebanon does not suggest that it is big, but straight and perfectly formed.

The man is not alone in finding his beloved to be attractive and worthy of praise. In 5:10-16 (NET), the maiden draws a picture of her male lover for the "daughters of Jerusalem." She follows the pattern of going from head to toe, then returns to his mouth:

> My beloved is dazzling and ruddy; he stands out in comparison to all
> other men.
> His head is like the most pure gold. His hair is curly–black like a raven.
> His eyes are like doves by streams of water, washed in milk, mounted
> like jewels.
> His cheeks are like garden beds full of balsam trees yielding perfume.
> His lips are like lilies dripping with drops of myrrh.
> His arms are like rods of gold set with chrysolite. His abdomen is like
> polished ivory inlaid with sapphires.
> His legs are like pillars of marble set on bases of pure gold.
> His appearance is like Lebanon, choice as its cedars.
> His mouth is very sweet; he is totally desirable. This is my beloved!
> This is my companion, O maidens of Jerusalem!

Here the word for "dazzling" (v. 10) is usually used to describe a shiny rock or piece of jewelry. "Ruddy" is from the word 'adam, which can mean either "red" or "man." Perhaps the maiden here intends both: that his ruddy complexion gives him a manly appearance. The NET's "he stands out in comparison to all other men" comes from the literal phrase "distinguished from 10,000," meaning that no one compares with him.

The "most pure gold" of his head does not suggest color or hardness, but value: his face is like gold to her, surrounded by raven-black curls (v. 11) and featuring eyes of bright color set into clear white (v. 12). The maiden's choice of imagery favors herbal scents and architectural or jewelry-based metaphors for his cheeks, arms, abdomen, and legs (vv. 13-15), but the return to his mouth in v. 16 suggests that she finds his sensual kisses to be especially enthralling.

For Reflection: *If you have a beloved partner, what imagery might you use to describe him or her?*

POEMS OF ENCOUNTER

Several poems in the Song relate to an encounter between the two lovers, either anticipated, or in the past. One example is found in the previous study of 2:1-15. Encounter poems may speak of both seeking and meeting. We find a series of such poems in the first chapter, arranged like a dialogue. The woman speaks first, and then her lover replies:

> Tell me, O you whom my heart loves, where do you pasture your sheep?
> Where do you rest your sheep during the midday heat? Tell me lest I
>   wander around beside the flocks of your companions!
> If you do not know, O most beautiful of women, simply follow the
>   tracks of my flock, and pasture your little lambs beside the tents of
>   the shepherds. (1:7-8)

Notice how the description of the male lover soon shifts from that of shepherd to king, while the maiden is no longer a poor vine-keeper (as in 1:5-6), but adorned with jewelry. The man speaks first (1:9-11), followed by the woman (1:12-14):

> O my beloved, you are like a mare among Pharaoh's stallions. Your cheeks
> are beautiful with ornaments, Your neck is lovely with strings of jewels.
> We will make for you gold ornaments studded with silver.

> While the king was at his banqueting table my nard gave forth its fragrance.
> My beloved is like a fragrant pouch of myrrh spending the night between
> my breasts. My beloved is like a cluster of henna blossoms in the vineyards of
> En-gedi. (1:9-14, NET)

Myrrh was a luxury item that had to be imported into Israel. It could be kept as a liquid in bottles, but was also mixed with fat and bound in a cloth sachet worn next to the body. As the fat melted, the scent of the myrrh would be released as perfume. Apparently, it was sometimes worn to bed, on a cord that dangled it between the breasts.

Henna blossoms could also be made into a sweet perfume, as well as an orange dye that could be used for body painting. En-Gedi was an oasis near the Dead Sea, a delightful garden spot within a dry and barren land.

> **A powerful place:** The reference to "my mother's bedchamber" in 3:4 is an image of feminine power: "I held him and would not let him go / till I had brought him to my mother's house / to the room of the one who conceived me." Does the woman want to have sex and potentially conceive in the same bed where she might have been conceived?
>
> A similar image is found in 8:5, where the woman speaks of making love under the same apple tree where her lover was conceived and born: as his mother had awakened him to life under the apple tree, so his beloved recalls opening his eyes to love.

Other encounter poems include fascinating elements. Chapter 3 is a study in contrasts: the first five verses describe a nighttime encounter in which the maiden leaves her bed to go searching for her lover, then brings him back to her mother's bedchamber. This is followed by an imaginative description of King Solomon's processional (3:6-11) and his elaborate palanquin, whose couch is inlaid with "love"—or with leather: the same Hebrew word is used for both.

This does not imply that the poem is necessarily about King Solomon, but that the two lovers can imagine themselves as royalty: they are the queen and king of each other's hearts. Recall that in chapter 1 they were first identified as a vineyard keeper (the woman) and a shepherd (the man) before speaking of their encounter as occurring at a royal banquet table.

Chapter 4 includes some intriguing terminology, for the man describes his beloved as both "sister" and "bride." Both terms are probably metaphors: the poem is certainly not about incest, and may not be about marriage, though some interpreters insist it must be so. At heart, the poem is about two people who cherish each other and are determined to enjoy each other. The sexual imagery is obvious. After the descriptive poem of 4:1-7, the male lover exclaims:

You have ravished my heart, my sister, my bride, you have ravished my
heart with a glance of your eyes, with one jewel of your necklace.

How sweet is your love, my sister, my bride! How much better is your
love than wine, and the fragrance of your oils than any spice!
Your lips distill nectar, my bride; honey and milk are under your
tongue; the scent of your garments is like the scent of Lebanon.
A garden locked is my sister, my bride, a garden locked, a fountain sealed.
Your channel is an orchard of pomegranates with all choicest fruits,
henna with nard, nard and saffron, calamus and cinnamon, with
all trees of frankincense, myrrh and aloes, with all chief spices—a
garden fountain, a well of living water, and flowing streams from
Lebanon. (4:9-13, NRSV)

For Reflection: *Do you find these passages offensive, or does it encourage you to know that the biblical message includes a deep appreciation for human sexuality?*

IMAGES TO REMEMBER
(8:6-8)

Among the brief poems and pleas of chapter 8, we find one of the most memorable images of the book. There, the beloved woman says to her partner:

Set me as a seal upon your heart, as a seal upon your arm; for love is
strong as death, passion fierce as the grave. Its flashes are flashes of
fire, a raging flame.
Many waters cannot quench love, neither can floods drown it.
If one offered for love all the wealth of his house, it would be
utterly scorned. (8:6-7, NRSV)

The "seal" of which she speaks refers to a small signet, usually a semi-precious stone, sometimes shaped as a cylinder, into which a design had been engraved. It was used as a stamp or rolled across wet pottery to show ownership, or applied to the blob of clay used to affirm authorization of a document. ⚑

⚑ **Seals:** This bulla—a hardened blob of clay that was once used to seal a letter—is marked with a seal reading "Belonging to Berachyahu, son of Neriah, the scribe." Berachyahu is a full spelling of the Hebrew name translated as Baruch, the scribe who worked with the prophet Jeremiah.

> 🔌 **Phylacteries:** The image of being set "as a seal upon your heart, as a seal upon your arm" calls to mind the Orthodox Jewish practice, described in Deuteronomy 6, of wearing phylacteries.
>
> During prayer time, Orthodox Jews tie small leather boxes containing portions of scripture from the Torah to their forehead and their upper arm using leather strips. This is a way of publicly demonstrating one's allegiance to God and to the Torah.

A man's seal was valuable and precious to him: he would not want to part from it. Some men wore it on a cord around the neck (where it might rest above the heart), in a signet ring on the hand, or as part of a bracelet worn about the wrist.

In essence, the woman is saying "Stamp me upon your heart, tattoo me on your arm," or perhaps "Wear me as the seal above your heart, as the amulet on your arm." The woman does not want to be separated from her beloved, but identified with him in a public and inextricable way. 🔌

In our day, wedding rings serve this same purpose: public tokens worn so regularly that they become part of us and constantly identify us as "belonging" or "sealed" to our spouse. Other pieces of jewelry might also bear significance as gifts marking an anniversary or another memorable occasion. They serve as constant reminders of our loved one's presence in our lives.

True love is persistent and permanent, both strong and ferociously devoted. The woman expresses this through the powerful affirmation that "love is as strong as death // passion fierce as the grave" (v. 6). Love, real love, is strong enough to endure any hardship and remain true. The ancients knew of nothing stronger or more certain than death, so it was not unusual to incorporate death into metaphors to indicate certainty. "The grave" translates the Hebrew "Sheol," thought of as a shadowy land of the dead that would eventually claim everyone.

The fire of love is so powerful that no waters can quench it, the woman declares, not even floods (v. 7a). In our media-drenched lives, we may be flooded by distractions and temptations, but real love will burn true and not be washed away.

Love is not only unquenchable, the woman said, but invaluable. "If one offered for love all the wealth of his house, it would be utterly scorned" (v. 7b). "Can't buy me love," the Beatles sang, echoing this thought. True love cannot be bought or sold because it is beyond price and immune to commercial transactions. One may pay for companionship or even sex, but love is not for sale.

Not everyone has the good fortune to have a beloved partner they could describe as beautifully as the poets who composed the Song of Songs, or to experience with another person love as strong as death and as fierce as the grave. If you have known that kind of love, celebrate it, cherish it, and protect it.

If not, perhaps your time for love will yet come. In the meantime, we all can appreciate the love of God that the rabbis saw reflected in the poetry of this book—a love that granted us the priceless gift of loving one another as well as loving God.

> **For Reflection:** *How do you respond to the imagery of "love as strong as death, passion fierce as the grave"? Can you think of other metaphors that might convey the depth and power of true love?*

THE HARDEST QUESTION
Is love passionate or jealous?

The Song of Songs is rife with translation difficulties, partly because Hebrew poetry is inherently tricky, but more often because the words used are rare: about 11 percent of the words in the Song of Songs do not appear elsewhere in the Bible. Thus, we have questions about whether the word *sharar* in 7:2 should be translated as "navel" or "vulva," and whether *galash* in 4:1 means that the maiden's hair "reclines" or "moves down" on the slopes of Gilead.

The issue in 8:6 is not a matter of rare words, but of relatively common words that can have multiple meanings. The maiden says that "love is strong as death, passion fierce as the grave. Its flashes are flashes of fire, a raging flame."

While I have favored the translation "passion fierce as the grave," the author may have intended an alternate meaning for *qin'ah*, which has the basic meaning "ardor, zeal, or passion." In certain contexts, it can refer to anger sparked by jealousy (Num. 5:14, 30) or competitiveness that grows from envy (Eccl. 4:4, 9:6).

The term is related to words in the Akkadian and Arabic languages, where it has the meaning "to be red," giving the idea of someone being red in the face due to the intensity of their emotions. While the translation "jealous" is traditional (so KJV, NIV, NAS), the poetic form places the word in parallel with "love," so some would argue that "passion" is a more apt rendering.

A related question has to do with the word's comparison to Sheol/the grave. While the NRSV has "passion fierce as the grave," NET has "passion unrelenting as the grave" (compare to NIV11's "unyielding as the grave"). The KJV, however, has "cruel as the grave." Why such variety? The basic meaning of the word in question (*qashah*) is "hard" or "severe," often in the sense of being unyielding. One can think of passion as determined and unwilling to let go, or of jealousy as

being a severe taskmaster. Some apparently understand this to suggest that love—
or at least, the betrayal of love—can sometimes seem quite cruel, but the author's
intent is clearly positive.

The closing lines can be cited to support either position: "Its flashes are flashes
of fire, a raging flame" (NRSV). Jealousy is often portrayed as hot or burning, but
so is love, and so is passion. While jealousy would be an appropriate response if
one's beloved should stray, there is no indication of dallying affections here: the
two lovers are completely engrossed in each other, their passions reserved for their
partner alone.

RUTH

Love with a Twist

Ruth 1:1–2:23
"YOU'RE ALL I HAVE"

Do not press me to leave you or to turn back from following you!
Where you go, I will go; Where you lodge, I will lodge;
your people shall be my people, and your God my God."
—Ruth 1:17

D o you like happy endings? Most of us do. While movies or books that end tragically may receive critical acclaim, most of us prefer a tale in which the main characters overcome threats and trials to find happiness in the end. That's one of the reasons the book of Ruth is one of the most popular stories in the Bible: it shares the typical features of a traditional folktale in which good people fall into trial and experience a major need that is ultimately fulfilled in surprising ways. ⬇

⬇ **Location, location**: Most Bibles have the book of Ruth appearing between Judges and 1 Samuel based on chronology: v. 1 sets the story "in the days when the judges ruled." By the end of the book, we learn that Ruth became David's grandmother, so there are grounds for having her story appear before David's.

Doing this, however, inserts Ruth into the middle of a larger unified narrative. The books of Judges through 2 Kings, except for Ruth, were put together in their current form sometime during the Babylonian exile (6th century BCE). Scholars generally refer to this block of text as the "Deuteronomistic History," because it provides a theological interpretation of Israel's history from the perspective of the covenant theology taught in Deuteronomy. In the Hebrew Bible, Ruth appears with the other Megillot in a larger section called the "Writings."

OF FAMILY AND FAMINE
(1:1-5)

The story begins with a happy family living in the land of Judah. The father's name is Elimelech, which could mean "my God is king." His two sons have names that not only rhyme, but also point ominously toward a mutual fate.

"Mahlon" appears to be from a root that means "to be sick," and "Chilion" could mean "frail." Why give children such names? Infant mortality was high in ancient times, and the boys may have appeared sickly at birth. It's also possible that the narrator attributed nicknames to them as a harbinger of their early deaths. ♦

The mother's name is Naomi, which comes from an adjective that means "pleasant," and could be translated as "pleasant one" or "sweetness." We soon learn that, though the book is named for her daughter-in-law, Naomi is the primary protagonist whose misfortunes drive the story.

We meet Naomi's family during a time of famine in their home village of Bethlehem—an ironic touch, since "Bethlehem" means "House of Bread," but there was no bread. Elimelech chooses to go in search of better prospects, taking his wife and sons to live "as sojourners" or "foreigners" in the land of Moab.

♦ **Names:** Biblical writers sometimes called characters by names designed to reflect on their character or reputation. The names of Eli's two sons—Hophni and Phinehas—are first spoken by a visiting prophet who condemned their greedy and immoral behavior (1 Sam. 2:27-36). "Hophni" is an Egyptian word meaning "toad," and "Phinehas" is Hebrew for "brass lips." Priests typically gave their sons theophoric names, including a version of God's name such as "*el*" or "*yah*" in them, so it is unlikely that Hophni and Phinehas were their given names.

Likewise, the Deuteronomists refused to call Saul's sons "Ishbaal" and "Mephibaal" by their given names. "Baal" means "lord" and may have been used with reference to God at some point, but by the time 2 Samuel was written, the name Baal was so identified with the Canaanite god Baal that it was considered shameful to have such a name. As such, the writer of 2 Samuel called the two sons "Ishbosheth" and "Mephibosheth," substituting the word for "shame" ("*bosheth*") in the place of Baal. 1 Chron. 8:33 preserves the original form as "Esh-baal."

In the book of Ruth, all of the names are significant and in some way reflect the character of the persons to whom they are attached.

Moab was not a far country, but located within a one- or two-day walk. While Bethlehem was located about 18 miles west of the Dead Sea, Moab was located on the southeastern side of the sea. Moabite and Hebrew are both dialects of the same northwest Semitic language family, so communication would not have been difficult. ♦

Soon after relocating, Elimelech died of unstated causes, leaving Naomi to care for two sons (v. 3). She managed to arrange marriages for them both, but would have had little to offer as a bride price, so it is likely that their wives came from poor Moabite families (v. 4).

The brides' names are also significant: "Orpah" could be related to a word meaning "clouds" or another referring to "the back of the neck," so we are not surprised when she later turns away from Naomi. Some believe the name "Ruth" is related to a word meaning "friendship" or "companion," but others argue that it more closely approximates a word meaning "well-watered," implying fertility.

> ♦ **Moabite cousins?** A story in Genesis 19:30-38 traces the ancestry of the Moabites and Ammonites to the daughters of Lot. After fleeing from Sodom, according to the story, Lot and his daughters were so afraid of the surrounding peoples that they chose to live in an isolated cave. The daughters, fearful of having no progeny, got their father drunk and had sex with him in hopes of getting pregnant. They each bore sons, the narrator says, naming them Moab and Ben-ammi. The Ammonites lived just east of the Jordan River, while the Moabites were located immediately south of them. The story may seem fanciful, but attests to a Hebrew belief that the Moabites and Ammonites were their distant kin.

Sometime later—it's unclear whether "10 years" refers to the total time in Moab or the time since following the marriages—both sons had died without siring children, leaving Naomi and her two Moabite daughters-in-law as widows (v. 5). In later tradition, the rabbis judged that God had cursed Elimelech and his sons with death because they dared to leave the Promised Land, but that is not implied by the story, in which their deaths serve to introduce the main plot.

Naomi is stranded in a foreign land, widowed and saddled with two daughters-in-law and no sons to provide for her in old age. Naomi's bereft situation quickly sets up the story so that we know what is necessary for a happy ending: she needs food, and she needs sons. Is there hope for Naomi? How will the crisis be resolved?

OF LOYALTY AND LAMENT
(1:6-22)

When Naomi heard that "the LORD had considered his people and given them food," she determined to return to Bethlehem, where Elimelech had owned property and she might appeal to extended family members for help (vv. 6-7). Knowing that she had nothing to offer them, Naomi urged her widowed daughters-in-law to return to their parents, take another husband, and find new happiness (vv. 8-9).

Both Orpah and Ruth demurred, but Naomi bitterly protested that she had no more sons for them to marry and felt cursed, for "the hand of the LORD has turned against me" (vv. 10-13). After some persuasion, Orpah agreed to stay behind and seek her future in Moab (v. 14). ⚘ Ruth, however, elected to remain with Naomi, eloquently declaring her love and allegiance: "Where you go, I will go; where you lodge, I will lodge; your people shall be my people, and your God my God" (v. 16).

⚘ **Orpah's future?** A later rabbinic tradition made the unlikely claim that Ruth and Orpah were sisters, both daughters of the Moabite king Eglon (*Ruth Rabbah* 2:9). Another midrash claimed that Orpah became promiscuous after leaving Naomi, and that the giant Goliath was born of an illicit union (BT *Sotah* 42b). Thus, while Ruth became the great-grandmother of David, Orpah was the mother of his nemesis Goliath. Such traditions have nothing to support them beyond the imaginations of the rabbis.

Many couples choose to use these words in their wedding ceremonies, often unaware that the pledge was first spoken by a widowed woman to her mother-in-law! Ruth promised not only to remain with Naomi for life, but also to forsake her Moabite gods and follow the God of Israel. Leaving no doubt of her intentions, she concluded with an oath: "May the LORD do thus and so to me, and more as well, if even death parts me from you!" (v. 17).

Seeing Ruth's determination, Naomi said no more, but led the way to Bethlehem, where the local women cried out in joyful recognition of a friend they had not seen in a decade: "Is this *Naomi*?" (v. 19). Naomi shared none of their joy, rejecting her old name ("pleasant one") and insisting that they call her "Mara" ("bitter") instead, "for the Almighty has dealt bitterly with me" (v. 20). Blaming her troubles on God, Naomi complained that she had gone away full, but Yahweh had "dealt harshly," "caused calamity," and "brought me back empty" (v. 21).

Despite her complaints, Naomi was not empty: Ruth was with her, and they had arrived "at the beginning of the barley harvest" (v. 22).

OF FOOD AND FLIRTATION
(2:1-23)

Chapter 2 is brilliantly written and designed to show how Ruth, a Moabite foreigner, became accepted as a part of the community and the clan. It begins with a digression in which the narrator introduces the reader to Boaz, a kinsman of Naomi's husband Elimelech—and someone who had the ability to reverse the women's negative circumstances (v. 1). His name could mean something like "in him is strength."

While Naomi remained self-absorbed and apparently inactive, Ruth took the initiative to find food. She offered to go and glean barley in the fields outside of Bethlehem, a practice that Israel's law afforded to both foreigners and the poor (Lev. 19:9-10, 23:22; Deut. 24:19-21).

Notably, Ruth said she intended not only to glean, but also to seek "someone in whose sight I may find favor" (v. 2). That expression usually referred to a specific person, and since v. 1 has told us about Boaz, we may guess that Naomi might have told Ruth, as well: she could have been hoping to find Boaz's fields and to gain favor with him. As the story is told, Ruth just happened to choose a field belonging to Boaz, and Boaz just happened to arrive in time to see her there (vv. 3-4). While their meeting appears to be by chance, there is little doubt that the narrator sees providence at work.

Intrigued by Ruth's appearance, Boaz asked the supervisor of his workers who the new young woman was by inquiring to whom she "belonged" (v. 5). In patriarchal culture, a married woman "belonged" to her husband and a single woman to her father. Boaz's main concern was to know if Ruth had any family connections.

The foreman identified Ruth as the young Moabite woman who had returned with Naomi. Noting her polite manners and determination, he added: "She has been on her feet from early this morning until now, without resting even for a moment" (vv. 6-7). This is often read to suggest that Ruth had been gleaning hard until that moment, but it could also mean that she had stood patiently by, awaiting the arrival of Boaz.

The foreman noted that Ruth had asked "to glean and gather among the sheaves behind the reapers" (v. 7). Ruth could have gleaned in the field without asking, based on her status as a foreigner, but could not "gather among the sheaves," where more wheat was to be found, without permission of the landowner. Could it be that her intention in asking the boon was to ensure that she would have an opportunity to meet Boaz and "find favor in his sight"?

The remainder of the chapter portrays a delightful and flirtatious interplay between Boaz and Ruth. Boaz spoke to Ruth as "my daughter" and urged her to stay in his fields with the young women of his household. He assured her safety, having instructed the young men not to molest her, and encouraged her to share in water breaks with the others (vv. 8-9). This was a kind response, but pointedly did not grant all that Ruth had asked for: the ability to glean among the gathered sheaves. ♙

> ♙ **Sexual tension**: Boaz's insistence that he has instructed the young men not to bother Ruth (v. 9), along with Naomi's insistence that Ruth remain in Boaz's fields lest other young men molest her (v. 22), introduces a clear note of sexual tension into the story. Evidently, activities other than harvesting were going on in the fields. In the next chapter, Ruth will visit Boaz in the field in the dead of night, and the tension will become even more palpable.

Even so, Ruth's response was dramatic and attention-getting: she fell prostrate before Boaz and asked "Why have I found favor in your sight, that you should take notice of me, when I am a foreigner?" (v. 10). Again we recall Ruth's interest in having the landowner show her favor (v. 2).

Boaz acknowledged that he had heard of how Ruth had shown such loyalty to Naomi by leaving her own family to care for her mother-in-law. Clearly impressed, he wished her God's blessing (vv. 11-12), but still withheld permission to gather among the sheaves. ♙

Ruth maintained her submissive approach, referring to Boaz as "my lord," hoping to continue "to find favor in your sight," and speaking of herself as his maidservant (*shifkah*), "even though I am not one of your servants" (v. 13). The term *shifkah* was used of household servants who were considered part of the extended family, so Ruth's word choice was a subtle request to be recognized as a member of Boaz's clan. Boaz's insistence that she remain in his fields, along with his continued show of hospitality, suggest that he did so.

⛏ **Sheltering "wings":** Boaz blessed Ruth by saying "May the LORD reward you for your deeds, and may you have a full reward from the LORD, the God of Israel, under whose wings you have come for refuge!" (v. 12). As we will see, though he attributed the protection to Yahweh, it is Boaz whose "wings" will provide protection and shelter to Ruth. The reader may still have this verse in mind in the next chapter, when Ruth visits Boaz in the field and asks him to spread his cloak over her (3:9).

At mealtime Boaz invited Ruth to come and sit with the household, dipping her food into the common bowl of wine vinegar, another suggestion that he had accepted her as part of the extended family. He personally "heaped up" for her so much parched grain that she ate her fill and saved the rest for Naomi.

Having observed her at work and considering her request, Boaz then instructed the harvesters to allow Ruth to glean even among the stacked bundles of grain where the pickings were best, and to intentionally leave handfuls of grain in her path (vv. 14-16). Ruth had not only found favor, but Boaz also appeared to be as interested in seeking Ruth's favor as she was in his.

With Boaz's intervention, Ruth worked all day, beat out the grain, and returned to Naomi with leftovers from lunch and "about an ephah of barley"—perhaps 30-50 pounds of grain (v. 18)—enough to provide basic food for weeks. Naomi's delight in learning where Ruth had been gleaning led her to speak more kindly of God: she blessed Boaz "by the LORD, whose kindness has not forsaken the living or the dead" (v. 20). ⛏ ⛏

⛏ **An answered prayer?** The narrator skillfully relates Ruth's return to Naomi at the end of the day (2:18-23). Naomi's dark depression lifted when she saw the amount of grain Ruth had collected, and she excitedly asked where Ruth had been. Ruth described the kindness Boaz had shown, but it was Naomi who realized that Boaz, "one of our nearest of kin," could be the answer to their problems.

One might expect things to move quickly from there, but the narrator retards the action by noting that Ruth continued to glean in the fields of Boaz throughout the barley and wheat harvests—usually a period of about seven weeks—but that she continued to live with her mother-in-law. If any further flirtation transpired between Ruth and Boaz during that time, it must be left to the imagination.

⚓ **Hunger:** The story of Naomi's need, Ruth's hard work, and Boaz's generosity are clear reminders of the reality of hunger and the pain that comes with it. Naomi's bitter demeanor changes significantly when Ruth brings home the raw grain she has gleaned, and especially when Ruth reveals the parched grain—ready for eating—that she has saved for Naomi. Earlier, Naomi had blamed God for causing her distress: now she blesses Boaz "by the name of the LORD" for showing lovingkindness toward them (2:18-20). Like Naomi, our thoughts about God's faithfulness may change with our fortunes.

For Reflection: *We don't have to be wealthy landowners like Boaz to make a difference in the lives of hungry people. Are there ways in which you have shown lovingkindness to those who face hunger? Is there more you could do?*

After explaining that Boaz was a kinsman, Naomi insisted that Ruth continue to glean in his fields rather than any other, and she did so, "gleaning until the end of the barley and wheat harvests"—time enough to amass a considerable quantity of grain (vv. 21-23).

With the end of chapter 2, the first element of Naomi's need has been met: she has food. But how will the second need be fulfilled? Naomi still has no sons to care for her in old age.

Fortunately, the book has two chapters yet to come.

For Reflection: *The narrator describes the meeting of Ruth and Boaz as if they both just happened to be in the same place at the same time, but it's apparent that he sees God's hand at work. Can you think of happenings in your life that appeared to be a matter of chance, but later seemed providential? Is there any way to tell for sure? However things happen, we still have our part to play in making the most of them, and thanking God for the opportunity.*

THE HARDEST QUESTION
Should Naomi have blamed God for her troubles?

As the story of Naomi's trials is told, she consistently attributed her misfortunes to God. In 1:13, she told Ruth and Orpah that "the hand of the LORD has turned against me." Upon returning to Bethlehem, she tells the women who recognized her: "Call me no longer Naomi, call me Mara, for the Almighty has dealt bitterly with me. I went away full, but the LORD has brought me back empty; why call me Naomi when the LORD has dealt harshly with me, and the Almighty has brought calamity upon me?"

Was Naomi correct? Had God, for some reason, turned against her and caused the death of her husband and sons? Some interpreters have argued just so, suggesting that God caused the death of Elimelech and his two sons because Elimelech showed a lack of faith in God by leaving Judah when times got hard and going to a foreign country rather than trusting in God to provide.

This interpretation has little to support it. Several stories in Genesis report that notables including Abraham, Isaac, and Jacob all left the land of promise for Egypt or other countries during times of famine, and none of them were condemned for relocating. Indeed, the Joseph story suggests that God intentionally placed Joseph in Egypt to provide food for his brothers and their families when Canaan faced a period of severe famine. Nothing in the legal material suggests that Israelites must prove their faith by remaining in the land during times of drought.

It was common in the ancient world for all things, good or bad, to be attributed to divine action. The "standard" covenant theology of the Old Testament, taught in the book of Deuteronomy, is that God blesses the obedient and curses the rebellious, but there is nothing to indicate that Elimelech, Naomi, or their sons had committed sins worthy of wiping out all male members of the family.

Had God arbitrarily brought such travail upon Naomi? Does God intentionally send bad things to plague good people? Such issues of theodicy gave rise to books such as Job and Ecclesiastes, and they arrived at no conclusive answer, other than that such things are beyond human understanding.

Do we want to think of God as one who purposefully sends disease to the innocent or who kills children to teach their parents a lesson? Are we to assume that human discipline and hard work count for nothing, with success or failure due only to divine fiat? Most people would reject such a notion, though some believers hold to the theologically unsupportable notion that "everything happens for a reason."

Whether God had intentionally turned against her or not, was Naomi wrong to voice such complaints? We should not be too hard on her. The Bible affirms what some have called a "theology of complaint," a God-granted freedom to express our pain and sorrow, even to question whether God has caused it. Job rightly raised such questions, as did Jeremiah in the Lamentations.

Having Naomi express her feelings with such brash freedom allows the narrator to depict "in somber and expressive hues the desolation, despair, and emptiness of the life of a woman 'left alone without her two boys and without her husband' (v. 5) in a world where life depends upon men."[1]

Where Naomi went wrong was to become so obsessed with her losses that she overlooked what she had gained: she was not alone or without support, for Ruth was with her, a daughter-in-law who Bethlehem's women would acclaim more worthy than seven sons (Ruth 4:15). Naomi's accusations against God may be theologically questionable, but they are understandable. Her failure to appreciate the love and presence of Ruth is a sign of a despair so deep that it had left her blind to the blessing God has given.

Naomi deserves our understanding. She lived in a male-dominated culture in which a woman's worth was measured by her marriage and her sons. As a childless widow, she was looking at the prospect of little status and a future that would be dependent on the charity of others. Perhaps we can forgive Naomi for not yet appreciating what a redemptive gift her Moabite daughter-in-law would prove to be.

NOTE

[1]Frederic Bush, *Ruth-Esther,* Word Biblical Commentary, vol. 9 (Thomas Nelson, 1996), 95-96.

AN ODD ROAD TO A HAPPY ENDING

Then the women said to Naomi,
"Blessed be the LORD, who has not left you this day without next-of-kin;
and may his name be renowned in Israel!"
—Ruth 4:14

Has your life worked out exactly as you planned or hoped when you were younger? Most of us experience unexpected twists and turns in life. Divorce happens. Jobs are eliminated. Loved ones die. Times change. Love grows—or doesn't. We may all have some concept of a dream life, but rarely does it work out as we had planned.

Sometimes life turns out to be less than we had hoped for, but often it becomes more. We learn that, though we can't say that all things are good, we can say that God is able and willing to work with us to bring something good even from trials, and often in unexpected ways.

A DARING PLAN FOR RUTH
(3:1-18)

Such was the case for a woman named Naomi. After traveling to Moab during a time of famine, Naomi's husband died. Her two sons married Moabite women but died childless, leaving Naomi bereft and fearful of a future with no family to support her.

Hope revived after she returned to Bethlehem along with Ruth, the widow of her son Mahlon. Ruth gleaned in the fields of a man named Boaz, who took a strong liking to her. Weeks of gleaning provided needed food, but Naomi still lacked descendants to ensure her social standing and future security.

How could that be rectified? Knowing that Boaz was related to her husband and perhaps aware of the sparks flying between him and Ruth, Naomi hatched an audacious plan. As a kinsman, Boaz could buy the property that had belonged to her deceased husband Elimelech and provide Naomi with financial security. If he also married Ruth, he could beget children to preserve Elimelech's posterity and Naomi's future.

With the harvest season ended, farmers turned their thoughts to winnowing the barley and wheat that had been stacked up in their fields through the several weeks of harvesting. During the hectic time of threshing and winnowing the grain, it was not unusual for both owners and workers to camp out near the threshing floor, both for convenience and to protect their hard-won bounty.

Naomi sought to exploit this seasonal sleeping arrangement to force Boaz's hand. One day, perhaps after Ruth had come in from a hard day in the fields, Naomi instructed her daughter-in-law to bathe carefully, put on perfume, and dress in her best clothes (3:1-3a). 🔱

🔱 **What did she wear?** While translations usually render the text as saying Ruth should put on her "best clothes," the Hebrew uses only the word *simlōt*, which could mean "festive garment," but more commonly means "cloak," a reference to the single garment that women typically wore. We learn later that she also had another garment, usually translated as "shawl," which she may have used as a veil or hood to remain unrecognized in the dim light, and which Boaz later filled with six measures of grain.

One might think she was preparing for a party, but it was more serious than that: Naomi was sending Ruth to the pallet where Boaz was sleeping in the field. Flirtation and sexual tension had hovered around the edges of the previous chapter. Now it comes front and center.

Naomi instructed Ruth to go to the place where Boaz and his workers were threshing barley, but to remain hidden in the darkness until she saw that Boaz had eaten his fill and become satisfied with wine before turning in for the night.

After observing where Boaz was sleeping, Naomi had told her, "go and uncover his feet and lie down; and he will tell you what to do" (3:4b).

What? Did Naomi really expect Ruth to sneak into bed with Boaz? Exactly—though just how far under the covers is unclear. Naomi told Ruth to "uncover his feet and lie down," presumably beside his bare feet, while waiting for Boaz to awaken and tell her what to do next.

The erotic *frisson* grows when we become aware that the word translated "uncover" was typically used with regard to someone uncovering another's nakedness, often in illicit situations (Lev. 18:7-19, for example). Moreover, in biblical Hebrew and in the ancient Near East, the word "feet" could mean exactly that, but it was also a common euphemism for genitalia (Exod. 4:25, Judg. 3:24, 1 Sam. 24:3). ⚑

Ruth followed Naomi's plan, presumably waiting until all were asleep and then quietly cozying up to Boaz (3:6-7). Should we be surprised that Boaz was startled when he woke up around midnight to find a warm and sweet-smelling young woman sharing his bedroll? (3:8). ⚑

> ⚑ **Which feet?** The text does not require us to read "feet" in 3:4 as a euphemism for genitals, but it allows it, and any Hebrew reader or listener would be aware of the optional meaning. The scene is highly charged: whether at his literal feet or a more intimate region, Ruth was to stealthily approach Boaz's sleeping place, pull back his covers, and lie down beside him. One cannot escape the sexual tension in the scene.

In the darkness he croaked: "Who are you?" Ruth replied, as Naomi had taught her: "I am Ruth, your servant; spread your cloak over your servant, for you are next-of-kin" (3:9).

The word translated "servant" (*'amah*, better, "handmaiden") indicates a higher status than "maidservant," which Ruth had called herself on their first meeting. A handmaiden was eligible for marriage: in essence, Ruth was proposing that Boaz take her for a wife and act as *go'el*, or "redeemer," for Naomi.

In Israel, when a man died, his closest kin had the responsibility of being a "redeemer" by purchasing his land and by accepting responsibility for the dead man's family. To marry Ruth, Boaz must also act as *go'el*. In that way, Ruth could maintain her relationship with Naomi, and Naomi's future would be secured.

We note that Ruth's response departed from Naomi's script: instead of waiting for Boaz to tell her what to do, she told Boaz what she wanted him to do: "spread your wing (literally) over your maidservant." And how would Boaz respond to this brash young

> ⚑ **Midnight visitors:** Why was Boaz so "startled" when he awoke to find Ruth sharing his bedroll? One possibility is that he could have thought she was Lilith, a night demon of Jewish legend who was thought to visit men at night and have sex with them: an ancient explanation of wet dreams.

woman who has crawled into bed with him and presented herself as a candidate for marriage?

The suspense is not long-lived: In a moment of high drama, Boaz expressed relief and praised God that Ruth had chosen him over one of the younger men who might have competed for her affections, a surprising setting for such religious talk: "May you be blessed by the LORD, my daughter; this last instance of your loyalty is better than the first; you have not gone after young men, whether poor or rich (3:10-11). ♉

Boaz knew, however, that one obstacle remained: another man in town was closer kin to Elimelech than he, and he would have first right of refusal (3:12). Boaz told Ruth to stay beneath the blankets with him through the night but move to a different place before dawn, lest anyone see them in a compromising position (3:13). ♉

♉ **Doing one's duty**: The custom described in Ruth 4 was called "Levirate Marriage," though Boaz reinterprets and extends the rule beyond its original intent.

If an Israelite man married but died before siring any sons, his nearest male relative (usually a brother) was supposed to marry his widow in hopes of begetting a son, who would have legal status as the scion of his mother's deceased husband, and who would inherit whatever portion of the family estate would have gone to his mother's first husband.

The overall intent was to perpetuate the name and heritage of the deceased while also providing for the widow and keeping her in the family (Deut. 25:5-10). The custom typically assumed that both the widow and her husband were Israelites. When Boaz announced that it also applied to Ruth, he was stretching the rule, but was sufficiently persuasive that no one questioned him.

Since performing such duties could decrease one's own inheritance, it was not uncommon for men to refuse to "do their duty." This issue played a key role in the story of Judah and Tamar that resulted in the birth of Perez (Genesis 38), who features prominently in Ruth 4 and is discussed further in "The Hardest Question."

When acting as a *go'el* for a young widow, a man was not only allowed to take her in addition to other wives, but also compelled to do so as a means of perpetuating the dead husband's line. Whether Boaz was a widower when he married Ruth is unstated, though his early flirtations and later elation at Ruth's offer seem to suggest he had been longing for company.

⛉ **What happens on the threshing floor . . .**: What happened in the hours between midnight and dawn, after Boaz told Ruth to lie down and remain for the remainder of the night, but leave before dawn? Kandy Queen-Sutherland approaches the question this way:

> Interpreters of the text often find themselves in "did they?" or "didn't they?" quandaries. Modern sensibilities cloaked in religious teachings that warn against premarital sex want the erotic scene at the threshing floor to fade into the shadows. Such sentiment demands that Boaz and Ruth remain chaste. They are merely two adults who spend the night together among piles of grain and nothing happens. Yet Ruth arrives in darkness and leaves before it is light. If the issue is propriety, then why not have Boaz send her away at midnight? Whether then or before dawn, it is still dark and that is the point. The text neither says nor denies what happens between them. Readers must respect that. The scene is erotic but not voyeuristic. What can be said is that what happens on the threshing floor is between adults, consenting adults. We can praise them for their self-control based on modern sexual mores, or we can leave them alone, hidden under the cover of darkness.[1]

By the time Ruth arose in the early darkness, she and Boaz were apparently betrothed. Boaz got up with her and filled her cloak with six measures of barley, apparently as a good-will gift for her mother-in-law, perhaps the promise of a larger bride-price to come later.

When Ruth returned home, Naomi was eager to know what had happened. "How did things go with you, my daughter?" (NRSV) is literally, "Who are you, my daughter?"—a question designed to learn if she was still Mahlon's widow, or had become Boaz's betrothed. After Ruth told her the news—the last words she would speak in the book—Naomi assured her that Boaz would settle the matter by day's end (3:14-18). ⛉

> **For Reflection:** *This passage from Ruth is one of many stories indicating that God is willing to work outside of accepted norms in order to accomplish a good purpose. Can you think of situations in which modern believers might be called to employ out-of-the-box thinking?*

⚓ **Six measures**: How much grain did Boaz pour into Ruth's shawl to carry home, instructing her to carry it on her back? The text says it was "six measures"—but which measure? An *ephah* of grain was probably about three-fifths of a bushel, and might have weighed 30-50 pounds. That's how much Ruth collected on her first day of gleaning, but she could hardly have carried six *ephahs* (180-300 pounds) in any fashion.

An *omer* was a tenth of an ephah, but six *omers* would be less than Ruth had gleaned on her first day, and seems too small. A *seah* was one-third of an *ephah*, which seems a more likely measure. Six *seahs* would have been about 60 pounds or more, a significant amount, but one she could carry on her back—even if she needed Boaz to give it a boost to get it in place (3:15).

A DRAMATIC PLAY
(4:1-12)

Boaz was as prompt as Naomi expected him to be. He went without apparent delay to the gate, where the town elders gathered and business was transacted before witnesses. ⚓ To no one's surprise, the narrator says the nearer kinsman just happened to be walking by as Boaz arrived.

Boaz invited the unnamed kinsman to have a seat, and called together the 10 elders necessary to witness legal matters. He reminded them that Naomi

⚓ **Bethlehem's gate**: Today, Bethlehem is surrounded by a thick security wall and high fences constructed by the Israeli government, restricting most residents to remain in their city, which today has expanded to encompass the towns of Beit Jala and Beit Sahour, along with refugee camps containing many thousands of people.

During the Old Testament period, Bethlehem appears to have been more of a village than a walled city with a typical gate. Even so, there would have been a main road leading into the village, and a small plaza or gathering place near the "gate" to the town would have been customary.

Elders of the city typically gathered at the city gate, where they or government officials decided legal cases, pronounced judgments, and witnessed business transactions. The judge's seat inside the Israelite gate at Dan was located beside stone benches for the elders.

had returned to Bethlehem, and announced that the late Elimelech's land was available for purchase (4:1-3). ♆

Sharply, Boaz reminded the man that he had first option to buy the land, though he had shown no prior concern for Naomi. The NRSV's translation, "So I thought I would tell you of it" loses the forceful imagery of the Hebrew: a literal rendering could be "I declare, I will uncover your ear"—an implication that the man had been deaf to Naomi's needs.

Boaz reminded the man that he could secure his option by declaring his intent before the witnesses. When the unnamed kinsman expressed a desire to buy the land, Boaz played a trump card, declaring that on the same day the nearer kinsman purchased the land, he—Boaz—intended to aquire Ruth as his wife, with their firstborn son to be the heir of her first husband (and Naomi's son) Mahlon (4:5). Another possible

> ♆ **Mr. So and So**: Names are always significant in Ruth. Since the nearest of kin decided not to redeem the land, marry Ruth, and carry on Elimelech's inheritance, the narrator chose not to honor (or embarrass?) him by calling his name. To preserve his anonymity, he had Boaz call him *p'loni almoni*, a playful—or possibly insulting—Hebrew way of saying "Mr. So and So." The NRSV and NIV11 use the unhelpful translation "friend," while NET has Boaz call him "John Doe."
>
> Kandy Queen-Sutherland notes that the man would have known of Naomi's return and her financial need. As the closest kinsman, he would have had primary responsibility for helping her, but had not shown his face until now. Boaz's greeting could be translated, "Well, look here, if it isn't so-and-so." Perhaps he didn't deserve to be named. Ultimately, he is revealed to be not only "*P'loni Almoni*," but a real "Phony Baloney."[2]

interpretation, based on a textual emendation and followed by the NRSV, is that Boaz told the man he could not buy the land without also taking Ruth as a wife, so that her firstborn son could gain his father's inheritance. ♆

If the former interpretation is correct, the man would obviously not want to purchase land that he could only use until a son was born to Boaz and Ruth. If we choose the latter interpretation, Boaz was gambling that the man would not want to add another wife to his household and thereby divide his inheritance. In either case, Boaz had him.

When the man declined to exercise his option, making it official through the custom of giving Boaz one of his sandals in the presence of witnesses, the way was clear for Boaz to declare his intention to acquire the land and to marry Ruth before the same witnesses (4:6-10).

> ⛨ **You, or I?** The *kethib* (written in the text) reading of 4:5 says "The day you acquire the field from the hand of Naomi, I will acquire Ruth the Moabite, the widow of the dead man, to maintain the dead man's name on his inheritance." The *qere* reading (a marginal note suggesting a better reading) says "... *you* will also acquire Ruth ... "
>
> In either case, the presence of Ruth complicates the matter. If the closer kinsman purchased the land, he would have use of it only until a male heir was born, who would inherit the land. This would be financially disadvantageous—especially if he bought the land but the son was born to Boaz and Ruth. It might also disrupt his family life. Boaz appears to have been rather wealthy to begin with. Since he wanted Ruth as part of his family, deeding over the field to the first son he had by Ruth would not have been a problem for him.

Boaz had shrewdly manipulated the levirate custom by extending it beyond Israel to include a Moabite widow, but was so convincing that the elders happily endorsed his approach: "all the people who were at the gate, along with the elders" affirmed the decision and spoke words of blessing to Boaz, expressing their hopes that the union would be fruitful in producing children.

The first blessing, "May the LORD make the woman who is coming into your house like Rachel and Leah, who together built up the house of Israel" (4:11a), suggests that the clan looked past Ruth's Moabite ancestry and adopted her into the family of Israel, no less so than Rachel and Leah, the daughters of Jacob's Mesopotamian uncle Laban. The wish that their children would give rise to a house like the house of Perez (4:11b-12) recalls an ancestor born to Judah through his Canaanite daughter-in-law, who also came to be appreciated in Israel (for more about Perez, see "The Hardest Question" on pages 50-52).

For Reflection: *Naomi's careful plans, Ruth's willingness to cooperate, and Boaz's happy acceptance of Ruth's offer would have been of no consequence if Boaz had not followed through with confronting the nearer kinsman and astutely working out the legal arrangements to make his purchase of land and marriage to Ruth possible. Have you ever made a commitment, but failed to follow through? Boaz provides a model for emulation: he did what needed to be done without delay.*

A NEW SON FOR NAOMI
(4:13-22)

Now we're ready for the happy ending, and the narrator relates it in short order. In the space of one verse we learn that Boaz and Ruth were married, Ruth conceived, and a son was born (4:13). That is no surprise, but what comes next may catch the reader off guard:

> Then the women said to Naomi, "Blessed be the LORD, who has not left you this day without next-of-kin; and may his name be renowned in Israel! He shall be to you a restorer of life and a nourisher of your old age; for your daughter-in-law who loves you, who is more to you than seven sons, has borne him." (4:14-15).

Note that the women did not congratulate Ruth, but *Naomi*. What is more, the storyteller says "Then Naomi took the child and laid him in her bosom, and became his nurse" (4:16). This does not necessarily mean that the aging Naomi became his wet nurse, though the author may be implying a miraculous supply of milk. In any case, it appears that Naomi took a primary role in caring for the boy she claimed as her own.

Note that Ruth has been pushed into the background, a reminder that Naomi is the central protagonist of the story: the women declared "A son has been born to *Naomi*" (4:17). And it was the joyful women of the town, the narrator says, not Ruth or Boaz or even Naomi, who named the child Obed, meaning "one who serves"—perhaps a sign that the child would serve to preserve Naomi's status in the community and care for her in old age, so she might live happily ever after.

With v. 17 we discover one of the primary reasons this charming story was included in the scriptures: Ruth's son Obed would grow up to become the father of Jesse, who would become the father of David, Israel's most significant and memorable king.

While the story concludes with the requisite happy ending, it also bears an important reminder that God delights in using unlikely people to accomplish great things. Elimelech's ancestor Perez had also been born under unlikely circumstances to a non-Israelite—a woman of Canaanite origin. Now we learn that Ruth, a Moabite woman, was to become David's great-grandmother.

While the story itself emphasizes Naomi as the central character, it is the foreigner Ruth who does the work of adopting and then adapting to a new family, a new culture, and a new religion. As Ruth succeeds in proving her faithfulness and her value at every step, her story could have borne a strong message in a setting, such as postexilic Israel, in which the Hebrews had become antagonistic toward immigrant peoples, refusing to welcome or integrate them into the community.

Given many Americans' less-than-welcoming attitude toward immigrants today, there might be a message here for us, as well.

> **For Reflection:** *The Old Testament law often emphasized the importance of welcoming strangers and making a place for immigrants within society. Does this story suggest something about how Christians should respond to those who come from places of danger or scarcity, seeking a better life among us?*

THE HARDEST QUESTION
What's the deal with Perez?

Perez is not a particularly familiar name, so why does he figure so prominently into the story of Ruth? Perez is first mentioned when the people at the gate celebrate the upcoming marriage of Ruth and Boaz, saying "… through the children that the LORD will give you by this young woman, may your house be like the house of Perez, whom Tamar bore to Judah" (4:12). After the birth of Obed and the resolution of Naomi's need, the book closes with a genealogy of Perez's descendants, from Perez to David (4:18-22).

On the one hand, then, Perez is mentioned because he is an ancestor of Boaz and thus of David. Of more interest, however, is that the births of Perez and Obed both occurred under unusual circumstances, and to a non-Hebrew mother.

The story of Perez's birth is found in Genesis 38, which appears to have been inserted into the longer Joseph narrative (Genesis 37–50) as a reminder that life continued in Canaan while Joseph was in Egypt.

Genesis 38 relates that Judah, the oldest of Jacob's 12 sons, moved away from his father's compound to establish his own household near Adullam, about 10 miles northwest of the family camp in Hebron. There he married the daughter of a Canaanite named Shua (v. 2). His wife is not named, perhaps because her role, as far as the story is concerned, is limited to bearing three sons and later dying at a propitious time.

Judah is not criticized for marrying a Canaanite woman, even as there would be no criticism for Joseph when he marries the Egyptian woman Asenath (Gen. 41:45). A later ban on Hebrews marrying outside the clan (see Josh. 23:12-13, Ezra 9–10, Neh. 13:23-29) had not yet developed.

Judah's wife bore three sons: Er, Onan, and Shelah. When the sons reached marriageable age, Judah followed custom and arranged for his oldest to marry a local woman, whose name was Tamar. At some point afterward, Er died, the text says, because he "was evil in the eyes of Yahweh," who "caused him to die" (v. 7).

Since Er had no children, Judah instructed Onan to "Go in to your brother's wife and perform the duty of a brother-in-law to her; raise up offspring for your brother" (v. 8). Onan, however, knowing that any son born to Tamar would get Er's share of the inheritance (and thereby reduce his own share), did not wish to impregnate Tamar. So, when engaged in intercourse, he practiced birth control by *coitus interruptus,* withdrawing before ejaculating (literally, "he wasted earthward"), so Tamar would not become pregnant (v. 9). Yahweh regarded Onan's behavior as evil, the text says, and caused him to die (v. 10).

Judah did not recognize the deaths of his sons as a divine punishment, but concluded that Tamar was poison. He did not want to take a chance on losing Shelah, his only remaining son, so he told Tamar to go and live as a widow with her father's family until Shelah was old enough to marry (v. 11). Judah's deceit became obvious as Shelah grew older, but Judah kept him away from Tamar.

Now the plot thickens: What is a desperate woman to do? In her culture, Tamar's future would be determined by whether she gave birth to sons. As a widow, with no children (like Naomi, several generations later), she would be doomed to a life of poverty, with limited rights. But Tamar was still bound to Judah's house and could not marry another. How could she have a son?

The death of Judah's wife (v. 13) gave Tamar an opportunity for a deceit of her own. Unwilling to accept a desolate future, Tamar disguised herself as a veiled harlot and set up a tent at a crossroads she knew Judah would pass on his way to oversee the shearing of his sheep, assuming he would be anxious for a sexual diversion (vv. 13-14).

Judah did not recognize Tamar behind her veil (v. 15) and sought to obtain her services, as the text boldly portrays with the explicit phrase "let me come in to you" (v. 16a). Playing the part of the harlot, Tamar negotiated a price of one young goat for the trick (v. 16b-17). Judah did not have a goat with him, but agreed to leave with her his personal seal with its neck cord and his recognizable walking stick as a guarantee that he would send payment later (v. 18a).

The deed is described matter-of-factly: "he went in to her, and she conceived by him" (v. 18b). Since she was no harlot, but only a woman seeking what was rightfully hers, Tamar changed back into her widow's clothes and packed up her tent as soon as Judah was out of sight (v. 19).

Three months later, it was reported to Judah that his daughter-in-law had "played the whore" and gotten pregnant (v. 24a). Judah, who remained in a position of authority over Tamar, declared that she should be burned (v. 24b), a penalty not called for in the Bible.

When someone was sent to bring her out for execution, however, Tamar had a messenger carry Judah's personal seal and walking stick to him with the message "It was the owner of these that made me pregnant . . . take note, please, whose these are, the signet and the cord and the staff" (v. 25).

Judah responded with appropriate chagrin, announcing "She is more in the right than I, since I did not give her to my son Shelah" (v. 26). The implication of the text is that Judah took responsibility for Tamar and accepted her back into the family, though the text is careful to point out that he did not have sex with her again (literally, he "did not know her again").

The real significance of Judah's soap opera story surfaces when the time comes for Tamar to give birth. Like Rebekah before her, she gives birth to twins, and the one officially born second becomes the most prominent. His name was Perez, and he became the ancestor of Boaz, as well as of David (Ruth 4:18)—and Jesus (Matt. 1:3).

The narrator reminds us that God works in mysterious ways. The story relies on legalistic elements (the requirement of levirate marriage, the penalty of death for harlotry) in some ways, but is surprisingly forgiving in others. Tamar is not criticized for her desperate act of pretending to be a harlot: indeed, Judah confesses his belief that "she is more in the right than I."

As with Tamar, Naomi's desperation led to a daring plan to have Ruth crawl into bed with Boaz to jumpstart a marriage so she could have sons.

The actions of both Tamar and Ruth suggest that sometimes one must go beyond the law in order to fulfill the law, even as Lot's daughters had done (Gen. 19:30-38).

By going beyond the expected and acting outside the norms, Tamar the Canaanite widow who feigned being a prostitute, Ruth the Moabite widow who played the seductress, and later Rahab the Canaanite harlot who hid Israelite spies in Jericho all reportedly became ancestors of David—and in that sense, of Jesus.

The actions of these brave women are named and noted as unusual, but not condemned. Sometimes, the story implies, being true to one's calling doesn't fit in the box of accepted behavior, but God has a way of bringing good even from the most messed-up of circumstances. The connection between Boaz and Perez, then, is not just genealogical, but also about the connection between Naomi, Ruth, and Tamar—women who dared to do what needed to be done for the preservation of their lives and heritage.

NOTES

[1]Kandy Queen-Southerland, *Ruth and Esther*, Smyth & Helwys Bible Commentaries (Smyth & Helwys, 2016), 124.

[2]Ibid., 148, 170.

LAMENTATIONS
Good Grief

Lamentations 1:1-22

SORROW
WITHOUT SURRENDER

How lonely sits the city that once was full of people!
How like a widow she has become, she that was great among the nations!
She that was a princess among the provinces has become a vassal.
—Lamentations 1:1

D o you enjoy books, movies, or television programs that depict dramatic situations in which it seems that all is lost, but the protagonists find ways to endure hard times on the way to surviving, if not overcoming the loss? We tend to like such stories better if they have happy endings—less so if the characters remain stuck in a world that appears bleak.

The Bible contains many dramatic stories, and many have happy endings. But there are also multiple accounts of suffering and hardship, conflict and war. Some of these stories appear as narratives, such as the good news of David's victory over Goliath, or the sad news of his surrender to temptation. And some of the stories are told in poetry and song: the Song of Deborah in Judges 4 and the Song of Hannah in 1 Samuel 2 celebrate victory and good times. The book of Psalms contains psalms of both praise and lament. Even the psalms of lament, however, tend to conclude with an answered prayer or an expression of confidence that deliverance is on the way.

But what do you do with a book that begins and ends with sorrow? Lamentations, as one might guess from the title, is the saddest book in the Bible. Its five chapters of heart-breaking poetry mourn the destruction of Jerusalem and search for meaning in the face of loss while pausing here and there to ponder the possibility of hope. The book's mournful subject matter does not naturally attract readers, leaving it as one of the most overlooked parts of scripture. Yet, we know that dealing with sorrow is a part of life.

Every one of us, if we live long enough, will suffer loss. People we loved will leave us by death or by choice, and it's hard to know which one hurts the worst. We may face illness or the loss of a job or financial struggles. We will suffer, and it behooves us to learn how to face hardship in healthy ways. ⍭

Could the book of Lamentations teach us something?

The poet (or poets) who wrote the five poems of Lamentations had reason to be sad: The people of Judah had been defeated in a bloody war, the proud city of Jerusalem set on fire, the sacred temple destroyed, and the country's leading citizens led captive into exile. Lamentations expresses such immediacy of grief that it was probably written soon after Nebuchadnezzar's troops razed and burned the city of Jerusalem in 587. It is one of our few sources of insight into what life was like for the poor Jews who remained among the ruins while their more affluent or influential countrymen were force-marched to Babylon.

Whether the poems making up Lamentations were written as a personal exercise or intentionally designed for a larger audience, it is likely that they soon came to have a liturgical use. Some scholars believe all or parts of Lamentations may have been read during an annual day of fasting amid the ruins of Jerusalem or among the exiles in Babylon, a painful way of remembering what had been lost—

⍭ **Lamentations**: The book includes what appear to be different streams of tradition, as indicated by Norman Gottwald in his brief commentary:[1]

- *A prophetic stream* that says the destruction is due to the people's sins: the image of Jerusalem as a faithless woman who has been defiled (1:8-9, 17-18, 20; 4:6), the corruption of deceptive prophets and priests (2:14, 4:13), the theme of judgment on sinful nations (1:21-22, 4:21-22), and the necessity of confession (1:18, 20; 3:39-42; 5:7, 16, 21)
- *A wisdom stream* that declares the mystery of God, that sees suffering as disciplinary as well as retributive, counseling patient hope in God (3:25-39)
- *A Davidic-Zion loyalist stream* evident in the words of observers who thought Jerusalem could not be defeated (2:15-16, 4:12), those who trusted the king as the "anointed" of Yahweh (4:20), and those who express shocked disbelief that the sacred temple could be so profaned (1:10; 2:6-7, 20)

and why. ♄ To this day, observant Jews read the book of Lamentations in worship services on the 9th of Av, the traditional date associated with the destruction of both the first and second temples. ♄ For this reason, in the Hebrew Bible, Lamentations appears as the third of five books called the *Megillot*, or "five scrolls," that are traditionally read at different Hebrew festivals.

We don't know who wrote Lamentations. The poems are anonymous, and may have multiple authors. An old Jewish tradition, picked up in early translations, ascribes the book to the prophet Jeremiah, who had such a hard life that he came to be called the "Weeping Prophet." Jeremiah was an eyewitness to the destruction of Jerusalem, though he was not among those carried into exile. A tradition recorded in 2 Chron. 35:25 associated Jeremiah with the writing of laments, and this apparently contributed to the idea that he wrote Lamentations.

Did he? We can observe that the book reflects points of both similarity and difference with Jeremiah, but we can't say more than that. What we can know is that whether Jeremiah wrote the book, or whether it was penned by a spiritually sensitive priest or temple singer or layperson, is not crucial for an understanding of the book. It's best that we don't know: the author intended to remain anonymous so that the laments could be read as representative of all the believing community rather than that of a single sensitive soul.

In Hebrew, the most common name of the book is *Eichah*. The word means "How?"—and it is the first word in the book and

> ♄ **Amid the ruins:** As evidence that worship or rituals continued to be conducted amid the ruins of the destroyed temple in Jerusalem, Jer. 41:4-8 describes a group of 80 men who came to the temple site in mourning attire, with their beards shaved and gashes on their bodies, to bring grain offerings and incense among the ruins. This would have occurred shortly after the Babylonian-appointed governor Gedaliah was killed, about 10 years after the temple was destroyed.

> ♄ **What was that date?** The Jewish tradition that the first temple was destroyed on the 9th of Av (the fifth month of the Jewish calendar; July-August on the Gregorian calendar) is an approximation: 2 Kings 25:8 says it fell on the 7th day of Av, and Jer. 52:12-30 says it happened on the 10th of Av. Later Jews dated the Romans' destruction of the Second Temple to the 9th of Av in 70 CE. Over time, the destruction of both temples came to be commemorated on the same day. The month of Av on the Jewish calendar usually falls within July and August on the Gregorian calendar most people now follow.

in three of the five chapters. In the Babylonian Talmud, the book is called *qīnōt*, the word for "dirge" or "lament." This was reflected in the early Greek translation, which called it *Threnoi* ("laments"), and the Vulgate, which called it *Threni* (Latin for the same). Thus the English name "Lamentations."

The most distinctive literary aspect of Lamentations is that the first four chapters are written as careful acrostics: each verse begins with a corresponding letter of the Hebrew alphabet, which has 22 letters. The fifth chapter is not an acrostic, but has 22 verses, reflecting a similar pattern. 🕎

A DESOLATE CITY
(1:1-7)

The first chapter—and the book—begins with the plaintive image of a desolate city: "How lonely sits the city that once was full of people!" (v. 1a). The author portrays Jerusalem as a royal woman who has lost everything, becoming not only a widow but also a vassal to a foreign king (v. 1b).

> 🕎 *Alef, bet, gimel . . .*:The most obvious literary characteristic of Lamentations is that the first four chapters are all neat acrostic poems.
>
> In chapters 1 and 2, each verse contains three lines, or strophes (except for 1:8 and 2:19), and the first line of each verse begins with a corresponding letter of the Hebrew alphabet (or *alefbet*). Thus, each chapter has 22 verses, the number of letters in the Hebrew alphabet.
>
> Chapter 3 has 66 verses, but is about the same length as the previous chapters. What is different is that all three lines of each poetic unit begin with the same corresponding letter (three lines beginning with *alef*, three with *beth*, etc.). When the text was divided into chapters and verses, the scribes numbered each line of the triplet separately. Thus, each of the first three chapters originally had 66 lines (if the extra lines in 1:8 and 2:19 are later additions).
>
> Chapter 4 is also a tight acrostic, different only in that it is made up of couplets rather than triplets, so each poetic unit has two lines, with the first line beginning with the corresponding Hebrew letter. Each couplet was numbered, so there are 22 verses and 44 lines.
>
> Chapter 5 is not an acrostic, but it is also poetic. It matches chapters 1, 2, and 4 in having 22 verses, and like chapter 4, has 44 lines.
>
> An interesting side note is that there were apparently different traditions regarding the order of the Hebrew alphabet. In the most common tradition the letter ꜥ*ayin* precedes the letter *pe*. In some traditions, however, the two are reversed. In Lamentations, chapter 1 follows the traditional order of ꜥ*ayin-pe*, while chapters 2, 3, and 4 reverse the order.

She weeps alone through the nights, with no one to comfort her, including former lovers and friends, who have turned against her (v. 2). The poet's reference to "lovers" may have followed the prophets' tendency to use immorality as a metaphor for idolatry. The prophets and the narrative literature accused the Israelites of going after other gods in addition to worshiping Yahweh. What they saw as "covering their bases," the prophets saw as a deadly syncretism.

The reference to "lovers" could also suggest the nation's pursuit of various alliances with other kingdoms, which the prophets also condemned as a lack of trust in God.

When Nebuchadnezzar's troops burned their way through Jerusalem, their victory marked the end of Judah (v. 3), the southern kingdom of Israelites. The northern kingdom (called Israel) had fallen to the Assyrians in 722 BCE. Though technically independent, Judah had been forced to pay tribute to the Assyrians and later the Babylonians. Nebuchadnezzar had initially defeated Judah in 597 BCE, taking many captives (including King Jehoiachin) but sparing Jerusalem and installing a new king who was ordered to pay tribute. Ten years later, Zedekiah's refusal to continue making payments—based on a faulty hope that Egypt would come to his aid—had instigated the final crushing blows against Jerusalem and the exile of many additional citizens.

With the city and temple destroyed and most of its population gone, the poet said "the roads to Zion mourn, for no one comes to the festivals." Judah's defeat had left the formerly bustling city gates desolate, the priests who would have led the ceremonies in mourning, and its maidens—who had a special role in the festival celebrations—grieving their bitter lot (v. 4). This verse names the city for the first time, using the term "Zion," which emphasizes Jerusalem's cultic role as the home of the temple and the center of worship for Israel. ⬩

> ⬩ **City names:** The author refers to the city by the cultic name "Zion" 13 times in the book of Lamentations, with three of those in chapter 1 and seven in chapter 2. "Jerusalem" is used just seven times, all in chapters 1-2.

Jerusalem's plight had come about because "her foes have become the masters," the poet said, a situation he ascribed to a belief that "the LORD has made her suffer for the multitude of her transgressions" (v. 5). ⬩ "From daughter Zion has departed all her majesty," the poet cried, with princes and people alike fleeing before the enemy (v. 6). Now the city was left with only memories of "all the precious things that were hers in days of old," for the city had fallen "with no one to help her" and with foes who mocked her weakness (v. 7).

> 🔯 **Heads, or tails?** "Her foes have become the masters" (v. 5) translates a
> clause that literally means "her foes have become the head" (*rosh*), with "head"
> used to mean the one in charge. This may intentionally reflect Deut. 28:13 and
> 44, where God promised to make Israel "the head" over other nations if the
> people were faithful, but "the tail" if they went after other gods and failed to
> keep the covenant. Israel's day as "the head" was over: now Babylon was the
> head, and Israel the tail.

For Reflection: *Think of what has caused you the deepest grief you have ever experienced. It might be the death of a parent or other loved one, the breakup of a marriage or cherished relationship, the loss of a job, a problem with your health, or some other sudden or tragic loss. How did you express your grief—vocally or silently? With acceptance or denial? What do you think is a most healthy way to give vent to our pain?*

A SINFUL CITY
(1:8-11)

Verse 8 echoes the prophetic judgment that Jerusalem fell because its people had "sinned grievously," failing to keep their part of the covenant with God. As taught in Deuteronomy and often echoed in Jeremiah's preaching, God had promised to bless Israel as long as the people remained faithful, but to punish them if they turned to other gods. The invasion and destruction of the city echoed the warnings of Deut. 28:52-63. The once-proud city was now mocked and despised, deeply shamed as all "have seen her nakedness."

Though she might try to turn her face away, the city's uncleanness clung to her clothing, evidence of a spectacular and appalling downfall before her enemies (v. 9), who had dared to ransack the city and run rampant even through the holy temple, where all but the priests were forbidden entry (v. 10). Now the city's residents were left groaning and desolate, as desperate for food as for a lost sense of self-worth (v. 11).

All of us face trials, and often our trouble is self-generated. Choosing to live beyond our means can result in unpayable debt and resultant poverty. Unwise choices of friends and the misuse of drugs or alcohol can result in addiction. Relationships fueled more by hormones than love can lead to troubled hearts and devastating developments.

Even so, we should remember that Christians do not live under the same covenant reflected in the book of Lamentations or the Old Testament in general. God has not promised to bless Christians if they obey and to curse them if they stray. Thus, while the author of Lamentations believed he could draw a straight line between Israel's sin and the destruction of Jerusalem, we need not think of every grief as divine retribution for our human failings.

Likewise, we cannot assume that God has promised to protect us—but we often grow angry with God when tragedies occur.

For Reflection: *Have you ever felt angry with God when tragedies happened to you?*

A MOURNFUL CITY
(1:12-22)

The second half of the poet's first lament focuses on the sad situation of the city and its people. "See if there is any sorrow like my sorrow" (v. 12) calls to mind the words of that mournful spiritual that emerged from the dark period of slavery in America: "Nobody knows the trouble I've seen, Nobody knows my sorrow" is a plaintive lament that speaks to the deep pain of one who has lost everything and must live in bondage to others.

The poet uses graphic imagery to describe the city's suffering: a fire from God that went deep into the bones, a snare that tripped the city and left it stunned (v. 13). Speaking in behalf of Jerusalem, the author imagined the people's sins as having been formed into a yoke that weighed heavy on the neck and forced them to follow the will of their captors (v. 14).

Yahweh had turned against Israel's warriors and allowed the city to be crushed like grapes in a wine press (v. 15), leaving its people with tear-stained faces and no one to comfort them (v. 16). Even neighbors had become foes, regarding the once proud city as nothing more than a filthy rag to be avoided (v. 17)

Speaking for the personified city, the poet acknowledges a belief that "The LORD is in the right, for I have rebelled against his word," resulting in the city's fall to its captors (v. 18). "I called to my lovers but they deceived me" (v. 19) probably reflects the city's attempts to stave off the Babylonians through ill-fated alliances with other nations.

The poet describes physical symptoms of grief familiar to any who have experienced deep loss, especially one that was self-generated: "My stomach churns, my heart is wrung within me, because I have been very rebellious" (v. 20). With death all around and enemies gloating (v. 21), the best the poet could do was to wish that those who had destroyed Jerusalem would come to a similar end. He could not imagine that the cruel Babylonians were guiltless, and though they had no covenant with Yahweh, the poet believed they were also subject to God's judgment: "Let all their evil doing come before you; and deal with them as you have dealt with me because of all my transgressions" (v. 22).

Christian believers who read these words may wonder what benefit they can find in them. We are neither Jews nor residents of Jerusalem. We live under a new covenant of grace through Jesus Christ rather than the old covenant of blessing or cursing based on faithfulness or folly.

What profit do we find in the poet's lamentations? We are reminded, first, that life can be hard: all of us will face the harsh realities of grief and loss. It is important that we learn the importance of expressing our grief in healthy ways. Weeping and mourning, crying to God and clinging to loved ones provide positive outlets for grief.

Many people, like the author of Lamentations, find it helpful to write about our feelings through journaling, composing an essay, or even through poetry. We need not think of every sorrow as God's punishment, but we do need to acknowledge when our own poor choices have contributed to the loss, repent of our wrongdoing, and learn to make better decisions in the future.

A particularly haunting aspect of the poet's mourning is that the city sits desolate, mired in sorrow with no one to comfort or help (vv. 2, 7, 9, 16, 21). May this poem challenge us to be sensitive to friends and acquaintances we know who may be suffering, and let it not be said there was no one to comfort them in their time of loss.

For Reflection: *When you have experienced deep mourning, what are the most helpful—or hurtful—things that others have done in seeking to comfort you? How can you learn from that in your own efforts?*

THE HARDEST QUESTION
Why study Lamentations?

The hardest question about our study of Lamentations may be why we should even bother. Lamentations is a book of sorrows that may seem more prone to depress than to inspire the reader: Why should we take the risk of studying a text that's such a downer?

Lamentations is included in scripture, but like many other parts of the Bible, is routinely bypassed in favor of more comforting texts. Why should we study the book of Lamentations?

Paul House, author of the Lamentations commentary in the Word Biblical Commentary, suggests four primary reasons why a study of Lamentations can be fruitful:[2]

1. Studying Lamentations helps us to appreciate the art of Old Testament poetry, especially poetry that addresses grief and hard things. "Taken together, the poems that make up the book of Lamentations display a linguistic and conceptual power rarely seen even in biblical literature," House observes, that makes them particularly worthy of study.

2. The study of Lamentations "could lead to a deepening of Christian scholarship and worship." Learning to appreciate prayers of lament is not only a scholarly exercise, but also an essential enterprise for those who believe the church has something to offer to those who cope with harsh and painful realities. A church that has become addicted to ease or focused on success has a lesson to learn: "Considering Lamentations could bring the church back into the real world depicted in Scripture. In Lamentations, sin is destructive; it must be confessed, or there is no forgiveness for it. In Lamentations, sin has consequences."

3. Since the book of Lamentations consists of carefully composed psalms of lament, a study of Lamentations can contribute to our understanding of similar laments found in the book of Psalms.

4. A study of Lamentations will give "depth, reality, and historical substance" to our study of Old Testament theology. "Closer examination of Lamentations may aid an understanding of the role of the exile, of personal frustration and pain, of liturgy, of faith, and of hope in the OT," House writes.

To House's arguments we might add the obvious truth that issues related to healthy grieving, the acceptance of personal responsibility, and the struggle to understand the ways of God in our lives are all important for our growth as mature persons, whether Christian or not. We don't learn about hard things without facing them. In studying a book like Lamentations, we can see how others have expressed their grief, engaged in self-examination, and sought to understand God's work in our world. The value of that is obvious. What are we waiting for?

NOTES

[1]From "Lamentations," *Harper's Bible Commentary*, ed. James L. Mayes, et. al. (Harper & Row, 1988), 648-49.

[2]From Duane A. Garrett and Paul R. House, *Song of Songs. Lamentations*, vol. 23B of Word Biblical Commentary (Zondervan, 2004), 279-81.

Lamentations 3:1-33

A DIFFERENT KIND OF HOPING

The steadfast love of the LORD never ceases,
his mercies never come to an end;
they are new every morning;
great is your faithfulness.
—Lamentations 3:22-23

If you've ever listened to much traditional American folk music or have seen the movie *O Brother, Where Art Thou?*, you'll remember the mournful song that begins "I am a man of constant sorrow, I've seen trouble all my days." ♉ Have you ever felt that such a sad ballad could be your theme song?

♉ **Constant sorrow**: The song "I Am a Man of Constant Sorrow" is attributed to a blind fiddle player named Dick Burnett, who published it in 1913 under the title "Farewell Song." Its roots may be deeper, though Burnett adapted the words. Through the years, the song was popularized by Ralph Stanley and The Stanley Brothers in the early 1950s and covered by artists as diverse as Bob Dylan, Waylon Jennings, and Rod Stewart. Joan Baez recorded a version as "Girl of Constant Sorrow," and Judy Collins sang it as "Maid of Constant Sorrow." Still the song remained relatively obscure until it was featured in the movie "O Brother Where Art Thou," which was loosely based on the sufferings of Odysseus in Homer's classic epic, *The Odyssey*.

The man we meet in Lamentations 3 could compete with Job as the original "man of constant sorrows." Indeed, that is how he introduces himself: "I am the man who has experienced affliction" (v. 1a, NET).

We've known sorrows, too. Can we learn from his glum tale?

WHEN ALL IS LOST
(3:1-20)

The first two chapters are lamentations over the fate of "Daughter Zion," the city of Jerusalem personified as a woman. ♦ The third chapter begins with a lament by the "man of constant sorrows," an anonymous person whose personal afflictions parallel and perhaps represent the suffering of the city.

And does he suffer! Using figurative language more commonly found in the psalms of lament, the man describes how one disaster after another has befallen him—all of which he believes are due to God's anger. Verses 1-9, as noted by Delbert Hillers, are like Psalm 23 in reverse: God is like a shepherd who leads the man astray, who pounds him with his rod, who locks him up in darkness, and who blocks his every move. ♦

> ♦ **Lament forms**: Lamentations contains both individual and community laments. In some cases, there are hints of a back-and-forth dialogue between the poet and Fair Zion, Jerusalem personified as a woman.
>
> The first four chapters all share in what Hebrew scholars call a *qīnah* meter, in which the second part of a strophe is shorter than the first. This gives it a halting, limping character that seems appropriate to the lament style.

If that were not bad enough, he portrays God as a wild bear or lion who has torn him to pieces (vv. 10-11), as an archer who has shot him full of arrows (vv. 12-13), as one who has made him a laughingstock and filled him with bitterness (vv. 14-15).

> ♦ **Turnabout**: As noted in the lesson, Delbert R. Hillers suggested that the poet's litany of complaints in 3:1-9 sound like Psalm 23 in reverse. Likewise, Hillers notes, the imagery comes across like "the opposite of the picture of salvation found in the Exodus and wilderness traditions and in II Isaiah; the vocabulary and imagery here are the same at numerous points, but turned to depict judgment, not grace."[1]

The sad result of such humiliation is that he has been left cowering in the ashes of the city, chewing rocks (v. 16). "My soul is bereft of peace," he says. "I have forgotten what happiness is" (v. 17). Even worse than the loss of happiness, v. 18 suggests that he had lost all hope of deliverance, leaving him with nothing but bitter and depressing thoughts (vv. 19-20).

For Reflection: *Have you ever felt like "the man of constant sorrow"? Has it ever seemed that the world had turned completely against you and that God not only failed to protect you, but also was the driving force behind the trouble? Does it feel that way now?*

WHEN HOPE IS FOUND
(3:21-24)

Given the morbid resignation of vv. 1-20, the affirmation found in vv. 21-24 comes as a surprise. Amid his manifold miseries, the poet remembers the central credo of Israel's belief about God, and in this he finds new hope: "The steadfast love of the LORD never ceases, his mercies never come to an end" (v. 22). ⬦

⬦ **Steadfast love and mercy:** The expression "steadfast love" translates the Hebrew word *hesed*, which "describes the disposition and beneficent actions of God toward the faithful, Israel his people, and humanity in general."[2]

The word translated as "mercies" or "compassion" is *raham*, a word that "signifies a warm compassion, a compassion which goes the second mile, which is ready to forgive sin, to replace judgment with grace."[3]

Paul R. House notes that the text reflects both Exod. 34:6-7, cited in the lesson above, and the promise of Deut. 30:1-11 that though Israel may sin and face discipline, God's compassion and willingness to start anew persists.

"Thus, Lam. 3:22 agrees with one of the most extraordinary teachings in the OT. Though Israel sinned against God through idolatry, immorality, oppression, and other forms of long-term covenantal adultery to such an extent that he finally punishes severely, the Lord will still start over with penitent Israelites. In other words, God's determination to bless and heal is as thorough and unusual as his determination to punish, if not more so. The road back to covenantal relationship may well be long and difficult, especially given the level of sin and the depth of punishment. Nonetheless, it is possible to begin."[4]

The poet's steadfast belief in God's steadfast love had its roots in Yahweh's self-description to Moses as being "merciful and gracious, slow to anger, and abounding in steadfast love and faithfulness, keeping steadfast love for the thousandth generation, forgiving iniquity and transgression and sin" (Exod. 34:6-7). That promise came in the wake of Israel's having turned to worship a golden calf: Despite the people's persistent idolatry, immorality, and oppressive behaviors, God was willing to forgive and start anew (Neh. 9:17; Joel 2:13; Ps. 86:5, 15, 103:8-14, 145:8). The prophet Jonah believed that promise so strongly that he cited the text to complain about God's show of mercy even to the Ninevites: "I knew that you were a gracious God and merciful, slow to anger and abounding in steadfast love . . ." (Jon. 4:2).

Despite his own sorrows, the poet of Lamentations 3 clung to the belief that God's steadfast love and mercy had not come to an end, but were "new every morning." In this belief he could declare "great is your faithfulness," a phrase celebrated in the memorable hymn by Thomas Chisolm, "Great Is Thy Faithfulness."

How could the man of sorrows come to such a change of attitude? Perhaps it is because he did lose hope—in his old way of hoping. If all his hopes were centered in God's coming to his rescue, he was bound to be disappointed. By shifting his hope from divine deliverance to the God who was present even in the dark, he found a new way of hoping.

"The Lord is my portion," he declared. "Therefore I will hope in him" (v. 24). The word for "portion" or "share" recalls traditions about the division of the land among the tribes of Israel. The priestly tribe of Levi was not given a section of the land because, God told Aaron, "I am your portion." Because of their service to God, the Levites would live in cities scattered throughout the land, and they would receive a share of tithes for their support, but their ultimate "portion" was in their special relationship with God.

The poet of Lamentations 3 had run out of hope when considering his disastrous life alone, but he found new hope when he considered that God had not forsaken him—that even in administering discipline or allowing misfortune to occur, God's steadfast love and mercy yet endured.

How we feel about life—and God—is a result of how we frame the experiences that shape us. It's important to remember that we don't live under the same covenant with God that Israel did: God has not promised to bless us or curse us on a sliding scale based on how faithful we are. Because of that, we may be less likely than the poet to attribute every misfortune to God's punishment for sin. We should also avoid the flip side, and not harbor unrealistic expectations of divine protection or grow angry with God when tragedy strikes.

Like the poet, we may find it helpful to lose our over-expectant hopes of supernatural safekeeping and learn to appreciate the present care of a God who goes with us into the dark valleys of life.

> **For Reflection:** *Think of the deepest loss you have suffered. Were you tempted to blame God, or did you fear that it was your fault?*

WHEN GRIEF IS GOOD
(3:25-33)

Having found a new way to hope in God, the poet's reflection led him to consider ways in which misery and sorrow could be reframed as avenues toward a positive outcome. He turns first to the virtue of patience, expressing faith that "the LORD is good to those who wait for him, to the soul that seeks him" (v. 25). Instead of complaining, he concludes, "It is good that one should wait quietly for the salvation of the LORD" (v. 26).

Trials can have educational value even for young people, the poet says. It is good that they learn "to bear the yoke" while they are young—probably meaning a yoke of suffering or hardship (v. 27). 🔅

The poet stresses humility in the next three verses, urging sufferers to find profit from sitting alone in silence, from prostrating oneself before God to the point of eating dust, from offering one's cheek to persecutors who would slap it (vv. 28-30).

> 🔅 **Good it is . . .**: The poet's manner of meeting the acrostic pattern in vv. 25-27 is to begin each verse with the word *tōv*, which means "good." In Hebrew, the verses would begin something like this:
>
> "Good is the LORD to those who wait for him . . . (v. 25),
>
> "Good it is that one should wait quietly . . . (v. 26),
>
> "Good it is for one to bear the yoke in youth . . . (v. 27).

Like the prophets and the authors of Israel's historical narrative, the man of constant sorrows believed that God could and should discipline the Hebrews when they deserved it, but he was convinced that God would not reject them forever (v. 31). Any grief God caused would be balanced by compassion and steadfast love that does not give up on people (v. 32).

The poet had no doubt that Jerusalem's destruction, Israel's exile, and his own sufferings were the direct consequences of divine discipline, but he did not believe for a minute that God enjoyed it: "for he does not willingly afflict or grieve anyone" (v. 33). Prior to a spanking, many parents have cited the familiar adage: "This is going to hurt me more than it will you." That thought is not unlike what the writer is saying here. He believes there is a time when God must punish, but he understands that God suffers along with the people.

A more literal translation of v. 33 would be "he does not afflict or grieve the sons of men from his heart." Our modern idiom would be "his heart is not in it." Punishment brings God no pleasure, but has the purpose of turning human hearts toward repentance and a return to right living (vv. 40-42). Divine discipline may be necessary, but God's compassion never ceases and God's steadfast love never falters.

For Reflection: *When one of the hymns in a worship service is "Great is Thy Faithfulness," can you sing it with confidence that God has been—and will be—faithful to you?*

THE HARDEST QUESTION
Who was the "man of constant sorrow"?

While the first two chapters of Lamentations are written mainly in third person (except 1:12-16, 18-22), the writer of Lam. 3:1-39 speaks in the first person. Verses 40-48 shift to first person plural ("us" and "we"), while vv. 49-66 shift back to "my" and "I." Some scholars believe these verses come from different sources, while others posit that one poet stands behind the entire chapter. If so, who is this "man who has experienced affliction"? At least six views have been suggested:[5]

1. Those who hold to the traditional authorship of Jeremiah would say, of course, that the man is Jeremiah. Some of the themes and vocabulary found in both Jeremiah and Lamentations are similar, but others are different. Like Jeremiah, the "man" of chapter 3 was convinced that the suffering experienced was due to sin. While Jeremiah is often mentioned by name in the book relating his prophecies, his name is never mentioned in Lamentations.

2. Others suggest that the writer is not Jeremiah, but one who speaks as if he were echoing the thoughts of Jeremiah as a model or paradigm for suffering. Persons such as Baruch and Ebed-melech were well acquainted with Jeremiah's message, and may have desired to express his views. The prophet did face considerable mistreatment during his ministry, but other than a similarity in language, there is little to commend this view.

3. Some have sought to identify the speaker with another biblical character, such as Judah's King Jehoiachin, who was captured and taken into exile, or his uncle Mattaniah, who Nebuchadnezzar put on the throne as a client king, renaming him Zedekiah. The connections between either of these and the writer of Lamentations 3 are not very substantial, however.

4. Another argument suggests that Zion, the city of Jerusalem, speaks as a personified man to describe the collective suffering of the people in individual terms. The greatest weakness of this view is that Zion is routinely personified as a woman in the rest of Lamentations, where the city is called "daughter Zion" or "fair Zion."

5. A fifth view is that the suffering speaker of Lamentations 3 is not a specific individual, but an anonymous "everyman" who uses the illustration of his own sufferings to speak on behalf of the people. This view fits with the book's apparent intention of keeping its authorship anonymous, though it doesn't explain how chapter 3 relates to the previous two chapters.

6. A final view, not very different, is that the "man" is a generic representative of all Israel. Though he speaks as an individual, he reflects the collective suffering of the community. Support for this view can be seen in the figurative nature of his language, which tends to describe suffering in metaphorical rather than specific terms that might relate to an individual.

While we cannot name the person who speaks in chapter 3, he is probably the same one who speaks in 2:11-19. It is likely, then, that the same poet who constructed the careful acrostic "set pieces" of Lamentations is also the voice behind the "man of constant sorrow."

NOTES

[1] Delbert R. Hillers, *Lamentations*, The Anchor Bible, vol. 7A (Doubleday, 1972), 65-66.

[2] *The New International Dictionary of Old Testament Theology and Exegesis*, W.A. VanGemeren, ed. (Zondervan, 1997), 2:211.

[3] Ibid., 3:1094.

[4] Duane A. Garrett and Paul R. House, *Song of Songs, Lamentations*, vol. 23B of Word Biblical Commentary (Thomas Nelson, 2004), 414.

[5] These suggestions are drawn mainly from commentaries by Paul R. House in *Song of Songs, Lamentations*, 405-408; and Delbert Hillers in *Lamentations*, 61-64.

ECCLESIASTES

Is That All There Is?

Ecclesiastes 3:1-15

IT'S ALWAYS TIME

For everything there is a season,
and a time for every matter under heaven
—Ecclesiastes 3:1

You've heard today's text before. Maybe it was at a funeral, where the reminder that there is "a time to be born, and a time to die" was intended to bring solace and order into a trying time. Perhaps it was in Pete Seeger's adaptation of the text, which became a hit song for the Byrds as "Turn! Turn! Turn!" in 1965. ♉ With the Civil Rights movement ringing cultural change and the war in Vietnam sparking widespread unrest, the song came across as a hopeful assurance that, if there's a time for everything, peace must be on the horizon.

You might be surprised to know that the person responsible for this memorable poem—the only part of Ecclesiastes that many people can recall—found little comfort in his belief that life is so ordered and predictable.

♉ **Turn! Turn! Turn!** "To everything (turn, turn, turn) / There is a season (turn, turn, turn) / And a time to every purpose, under heaven ..." Here's the URL for the Byrds' cover song: www.songfacts.com/detail.php?id=246. Seeger claimed that he leafed through the Bible and wrote the song in 15 minutes after his publisher complained that he couldn't sell the protest songs that Seeger preferred.

⬦ **Qoheleth:** The book we call "Ecclesiastes" was written by a man who tells us his name was Qoheleth, an unusual name formed from the feminine form of the *qal* active participle of the verb *qahal*, which means something like "to assemble." In that sense, it may mean something akin to "one who assembles," or "convener." The feminine ending was sometimes used to indicate a title rather than a personal name.

The notion of Qoheleth as one who assembles a group led the Septuagint translators to use the equivalent Greek word, *Ecclesiastes*. This is related to the term *ekklesia*, the Greek word often used for the church (the letters "c" and "k" represent the same Greek letter *kappa*; there have been different systems of transliteration). Perhaps this connection, and the notion that Qoheleth's purpose was to address the assembly, inspired the fourth-century Latin scholar Jerome to call him *Concianator*, and Martin Luther to use the German word *Prediger*, both meaning something similar to "preacher," as reflected in the King James Version.

Most readers would not think Qoheleth was much of a preacher. Qoheleth appears to be a sage, perhaps a philosopher of sorts whose reflections on life were often at odds with traditional teaching, but nevertheless drew an audience and were considered valuable enough to be preserved as scripture.

A CLASSIC POEM
(3:1-8)

The author of Ecclesiastes, who called himself Qoheleth, does not come across as a happy man. ⬦ An old tradition identifies the author as Solomon, but David's son could hardly have written Ecclesiastes. It is likely that the author was a person of some means, but not the richest man who ever lived, though he pretended to be in a brief royal fiction designed to emphasize his frustration with life (1:12–2:26).

Qoheleth began and ended his writing with a motto most familiar from the King James Version: "Vanity of vanities, says the Preacher, vanity of vanities. All is vanity" (1:2, 12:8). ⬦

⬦ **Editorial comments:** Ecclesiastes 1:1 and 12:9-12 were almost certainly added by a later hand, someone who sought to balance Qoheleth's radical cynicism and *carpe diem* musings with more traditional beliefs. The presence of the same sentence in 1:2 and 12:8 appears to have been intentional bracketing, Qoheleth's way of underscoring his belief that humans might find some joy and profit in life, but were unable to obtain deeper meaning or understand God's ways.

The word translated "vanity" is the Hebrew word *hevel*, which describes a breath or vapor that quickly disappears, as on a cold day. Some translators render *hevel* with words such as "meaninglessness" or "absurdity." Robert Alter's translation lets the metaphor speak for itself without interpretation: "Merest breath, said Qoheleth. Merest breath. All is mere breath."[1]

Qoheleth was not a typical wisdom teacher, though he wrote beautifully, mostly in a sort of lyric prose that occasionally morphed into poetry. He began his loosely organized teachings with a reflection on the futility of life (1:3-11): generations of people, like seasons of the year, come and go. The sun comes up and goes down, while cycles of wind and weather repeat themselves year after year. All the streams run to the sea, but the sea is never full. People live only to be forgotten, he concluded.

The old sage followed that reflection by portraying himself as a rich and powerful king who could do anything or have anything he wanted. After various adventures in excess—the sort of things people might expect to make for a happy life—he concluded there was nothing new under the sun and nothing to be gained from human toil, for "all was vanity and a chasing after wind" (2:11).

> ⚑ **Every matter:** In the phrase, "a time for every matter under heaven," the word translated as "matter" is *hēphets*, which often means "delight," "desire," "pleasure," or even "precious stones." The same word is translated as "pleasure" in Eccl. 5:4 and 12:1, and as "pleasing" in 12:10. It can also mean something as mundane as "matter," however, and context requires that translation here, as in Eccl. 3:17, 5:8, and 8:6.

That pessimistic note brought Qoheleth to the first formal poetry in his book. Whether he composed it himself or quoted previously existing verse is unknown. The poem explores the notion of a time and season for everything (vv. 3-8). ⚑ It consists of 14 antithetical pairs arranged into seven couplets in which the first and second lines are related. Each pair includes two things that seem mutually exclusive at any given moment, but all of which are common life experiences.

There is "a time to be born and a time to die," the poet said, "a time to plant, and a time to pluck up what is planted" (v. 2). Like crops that are sown and later harvested, human life is marked with a beginning and an ending. No one is exempt.

Verse 3 reflects a reality of human culture in which conflict seems inevitable, so that there is "a time to kill, and a time to heal; a time to break down, and a time to build up" (v. 4). The terms for breaking down and building up are drawn from construction, especially the building or breaking down of protective walls

> 🔯 **Wordplay:** In v. 4 the poet utilizes a playful combination of words that share similar sounds. "Weeping" and "laughing" are *libkōt* and *lisḥōq*, while the words for "mourning" and "dancing" are *sepōd* and *reqōd*.

(Isa. 5:5, 49:7; Ps. 80:12). Neither killing people nor destroying good walls is desirable, but in this world it happens.

Both weeping and laughter have their appropriate places and times, often related to mourning and dancing (v. 4). There is much in this world to make us sad or melancholy, but also much to cause rejoicing. Neither puritanical seriousness nor excessive frivolity would fit Qoheleth's reality, in which both sorrow and gladness have their place. 🔯

The imagery of v. 5 has given rise to much speculation. The poet compares times for throwing or gathering stones to "a time to embrace, and a time to refrain from embracing." Farmers typically cleared stones from a field to prepare for planting (Isa. 5:2), often using them to build a protective wall. A war story in 2 Kgs. 3:19, 25 reflects a custom of damaging enemies' fields by throwing stones into them, but neither custom has an apparent connection with human hugs or the lack of them. Rabbinic interpreters took "throwing stones" as a euphemism for ejaculation during sexual intercourse, and "gathering stones" as a reference to periodic abstinence.[2] 🔯 The remainder of the poem avoids metaphors, but this interpretation offers an apt comparison to embracing another, or refraining.

> 🔯 **Midrash**: Within Judaism, a primary role of the rabbis has been the interpretation of scriptures found in the Hebrew Bible. From the early centuries of the Common Era, rabbinic interpretations have been collected into works such as the *Mishnah* and the *Midrashim*. The *Midrash Rabbah* ("Great Midrash") on Qoheleth probably dates back at least to the seventh century CE.

Verse 6 contrasts seeking and losing with keeping and throwing away. On the surface, both relate to personal property. If something has been lost, there is a time to seek it, but also a time to give it up as lost. As possessions of differing values or usefulness pile up in our homes, we must decide what to keep and what to discard. One might extend the truism to abstractions such as ambition or love: there is a time to go after something (or someone), and a time to let go. That may be beyond the poet's intent, however.

The opposing pairs of ripping/sewing and silence/speaking (v. 7) may seem unrelated until we recall that tearing one's garments was a public symbol of

> 🔱 **Chiasm:** Some interpreters see a structure within the poem that literary scholars call a chiasm: various thematic elements that appear in one part of the text are balanced by similar statements found later in the text, in reverse order. A line drawn along the left side of each line would look like the left half of the Greek letter *chi* (X), hence the name "chiasm." Recognizing the elements of chiasm in vv. 2-8 reinforces the view that in v. 7, which corresponds to v. 4, the rending of clothes should be seen as a symbol of mourning.
>
> vv. 2-3: Life and death, killing and healing
>   v. 4: Mourning and joy
>   v. 5: Throwing away and gathering
>   v. 6: Throwing away and gathering
>   v. 7: Mourning (ripping clothes) and silence
> v. 8: Love and hate, war and peace

mourning (see Gen. 37:29, 34; 2 Sam. 1:11-12; 2 Kgs. 2:11-12; Job 1:20; and others). Clothes were hand-spun, hand-woven, hand-cut, and hand-sewn. They were not easily replaced, so when mourning was over, torn clothing would be repaired. Perhaps the poet also had in mind the loud ululations and other cries of grief that often accompany mourning: a time would come when trauma's weeping would give way to a quieter spirit. 🔱

The poem concludes with a more obvious pair of antithetical behaviors: "a time to love and a time to hate; a time for war and a time for peace" (v. 8). We would like to live in a world where love and peace thrive, but the cold reality is that there are things that inspire hatred, and there are times when war is not only the lesser of two evils, but appears to be necessary to preserve the liberty to enjoy peace and love.

> **For Reflection***: If you were writing a poem similar to the one in this Ecclesiastes passage, what antithetical pairs might you list? A time for work and a time for play, perhaps? Can you think of other things that reflect the reality of your life?*

AN ETERNAL PUZZLE
(3:9-15)

While the poet's ponderings on time and human actions may be assuring to readers, it was no comfort to Qoheleth. God is not mentioned in the poem, but

Qoheleth presumed that God had set the world and its realities in place, leaving humans to live in a situation they could not understand.

Human toil (v. 9) could be a reference to the ordinary activities of going through life, "the business that God has given to everyone to be busy with" (v. 10): Qoheleth wondered what gain or profit anyone could find at the end of it. While there was a time for everything, it was God who "made everything suitable for its time," not humans (v. 11a). As in 1:4-11, where he bemoaned the cyclical nature of life, Qoheleth knew that he might bounce between mourning and dancing or tearing down and building up, but if it was God who determined the times, Qoheleth could see no gain in it.

The real kicker for Qoheleth, however, was that God "has put a sense of past and future into their minds, yet they cannot find out what God has done from the beginning to the end" (v. 11b). The NRSV's "past and future" translates a word that usually means "eternity," and the phrase "a sense of" is not in the text, but added for clarity. A more literal translation could be "eternity, too, he has put in their hearts, but so that humans cannot find out what God has done from beginning to end." ⬇

⬇ **Eternity, or ignorance?** The Hebrew text was written without vowels, which were added many centuries later, based on the way rabbis commonly pronounced the text at that time. Some scholars believe the word '*ōlam* in v. 11 should be read with different vowels, as '*elem*, which can mean "darkness." Thus, they would translate the verse to say that God has put darkness or ignorance into human hearts, so they cannot understand what God is doing (see, for example, NET).

Perhaps Qoheleth's frustration was a belief that God had given humans an innate sense of eternity—of a divine reality beyond one's days of earthly toil—but had not given them an ability to understand it more fully.

This led the sage to find some comfort in the pleasures of life that he *could* understand: "I know that there is nothing better for them than to be happy and enjoy themselves as long as they live; moreover, it is God's gift that all should eat and drink and take pleasure in all their toil" (vv. 12-13; see also 2:24, 5:18-19, 8:15, 9:7-10).

Qoheleth's philosophy was not limited to "eat, drink, and be merry," but he firmly believed God intended for humans to enjoy what pleasures they could, even if they could not understand the full meaning of their existence. Trying to comprehend God's work leads more to awe than to understanding (v. 14), for only God can stand in the present while seeing into the past and the future (v. 15). The human task is to reverence God and appreciate the lives God has given.

This may seem depressing, but Qoheleth was skeptical of the prophets, and lived long before the time of Jesus. If he had known the gospel message of eternal life through Christ that we learn from the New Testament, do you think he would have sung a different tune?

For Reflection: *Consider Qoheleth's contention that God has "put a sense of eternity" in human hearts. Can you identify with that inner sense that there is more to life than what we experience on earth? Given that we live on the other side of the Christ event, do you believe you have a better sense of "what God is up to" than Qoheleth did?*

THE HARDEST QUESTION
Why couldn't Solomon have written Ecclesiastes?

Earlier we indicated that the book of Ecclesiastes appears to have been written sometime during the postexilic period. Modern scholars hold differing opinions of whether Qoheleth lived during the rule of the Persians (538–333 BCE), or after Alexander the Great conquered Palestine in 333 BCE, bringing the area under Greek rule and expanding the influence of Hellenistic thought. There are few, however, who would date the book earlier than 400–350 BCE.

But what about the traditional belief, held by many, that Solomon was the author? This came about because of the superscription in 1:1 ("The words of the Teacher, the son of David, king in Jerusalem") and 1:12–2:26, where Qoheleth employs the literary device of royal fiction as a teaching method.

It is unlikely that Qoheleth expected anyone to believe he was "king of Israel in Jerusalem," though countless people have done so, including the person who added the superscription and identified him as a "son of David," since all the kings who ruled in Jerusalem were Davidic descendants. Solomon, of course, also had a reputation for great wisdom, so it is not surprising that a tradition arose that Solomon was the author of this book as well as Proverbs, even though much of Ecclesiastes is contradictory to the traditional wisdom of Proverbs, which contains attributions to a variety of authors.

Solomon, however, could hardly have written the Book of Ecclesiastes. Why?

First, the royal fiction is found only in a small part of the book. In most of the book Qoheleth makes no pretension about being king. In fact, his attitude toward kingship is more critical than friendly. He sometimes connects kingship with injustice (3:16; 4:1-2, 5:7) and often makes comments about how to deal with kings, but not how to rule (8:2-4; 10:4-7, 16-17, 20). A king would hardly write in this way.

Secondly, the themes and language of the book are manifestly unlike what one would expect from a book written in the 10th century, as it would have to be if Solomon was the author. The Hebrew text has all the characteristics of the post-exilic period, a time when the Hebrew language showed influence from Aramaic, which had become the *lingua franca* of the period. The presence of Aramaic and Persian loan words is strong evidence that the work was written in a later period. Qoheleth's grammar is unlike classical Hebrew and has often been described as reflecting the transition period between biblical Hebrew and the Mishnaic Hebrew of the rabbis that developed in the last couple of centuries before Christ. Perhaps Franz Delitzsch said it best: "If the Book of Koheleth were of old Solomonic origin, then there is no history of the Hebrew language."[3]

Thus, there is little to substantiate the idea that Qoheleth and Solomon were the same person. Qoheleth could pretend to be Solomon for the sake of teaching his students, even as a modern preacher might present a dramatic monologue in the guise of an ancient prophet, but he was a sage from a much later period. Qoheleth's background and occupation are unclear. He appears to have been a person of some means—and frustrated that he could not take his wealth with him—but he was neither a king nor the richest man who ever lived.

NOTES

[1]Robert Alter, *The Wisdom Books: Job, Proverbs, and Ecclesiastes* (W. W. Norton, 2010), 346.

[2]*Midrash Rabbah Qoheleth* 3.5.1.

[3]Cited by Roland E. Murphy in *Ecclesiastes*, vol. 23A, Word Biblical Commentary (Zondervan, 1992), xxvii.

Ecclesiastes 1:2, 12-14; 2:18-23; 9:7-10

SEIZE THE DAY—EVERY DAY

Go, eat your bread with enjoyment, and drink your wine with a merry heart;
for God has long ago approved what you do.
—Ecclesiastes 9:7

Perhaps you've heard the expression *"carpe diem"* in a literature class, or maybe you've encountered it on someone's T-shirt. The Latin expression goes back at least as far as the Latin poet Horace. In Book One of his *Odes,* which dates to 23 BCE, he observes that one cannot know what the future will bring, and concludes it is best to "Be wise, and mix the wine, since time is short: limit that far-reaching hope. The envious moment is flying now, now, while we're speaking: Seize the day, place in the hours that come as little faith as you can." 🕎

The expression gained popularity from *Dead Poets Society,* the 1989 movie in which Robin Williams played the role of English teacher John Keating. Striving to get students in his all-male high school engaged, he famously said *"Carpe diem.* Seize the day, boys. Make your lives extraordinary."

> 🕎 *Carpe diem*: The translation cited from Horace's Odes 1:11 is provided by A. S. Kline, 2003, at www.poetryintranslation.com/ PITBR/Latin/HoraceOdesBkI. htm#anchor_Toc39402017.

The sentiment expressed by *carpe diem* did not originate with Horace, but has much deeper roots, as we shall see. One of those roots emerges from the Bible and the work of Qoheleth (more popularly known as Ecclesiastes), a frustrated and complicated sage whose writings bring an esoteric twist to the biblical message.

IS LIFE WORTH THE TROUBLE?

Trying to summarize the meaning of Qoheleth is like putting pantyhose on a cat: the book resists the effort, and any argument will probably have a few runs or holes in it. One way to approach an understanding of the book is by focusing on some of Qoheleth's favorite words and concepts, an approach the late Roland Murphy took in his excellent commentary on the book.[1]

Qoheleth's central and most-remembered theme is that of **vanity** (*hevel*). The term appears 37 or 38 times in Qoheleth (in one appearance the text is questionable). The repetition is evident in both Hebrew and English: *"Hevel hevelim, amar Qoheleth: hevel hevelim—hacōl hevel"*— or, "Vanity of vanities!" says Qoheleth. "Vanity of vanities! All is vanity!"

> ⛉ **A short life:** In the familiar story of Cain and Abel from Genesis 4, the name rendered in English as "Abel" is the same Hebrew word, *hevel*, that Qoheleth used to describe life as confounding or meaningless. In Genesis, the name provides a literary foreshadowing of Abel's destiny: seeing the name *"Hevel,"* a Hebrew reader would not expect Abel to have a long life.

In its most basic meaning, the word *hevel* means "breath," or "vapor." It could describe the morning mist that quickly burns away, or the breath one can see on a cold day that immediately disappears. Some have translated it with words such as "absurd," not in the sense of "ridiculous," but as something that is "incomprehensible." ⛉

Some writers think Qoheleth intended to suggest "meaninglessness," and often that seems to be Qoheleth's quandary. Whether he toils for wisdom or wealth, in the end, he sees no reward, no profit, no advantage—and that doesn't make sense to him. What's the point?

This brings us to a second important word: **profit** (*yitrōn*). After his initial statement, the second thing Qoheleth declares is a question: he wonders what profit one might gain from his or her toil "under the sun," that is, in this life on earth (1:3).

Qoheleth is the only biblical author to use the term *yitrōn*. It means something like "surplus," or "what is left over." He is asking, "At the end of the day, what difference does it make how hard you work or how much wisdom you gain—since you're going to die anyway?

Fortunately, Qoheleth does not end it there. He sees no lasting "profit," but he does conclude that humans can obtain a *portion* (*heleq*) to enjoy during their lives. We find this word scattered through the book (2:10, 21; 3:22; 5:17-18; 9:6, 9; 11:2). Qoheleth recognizes that some portion of pleasure or enjoyment of life is possible during one's years under the sun, and he calls on his readers to recognize and enjoy this "portion" and be grateful to God for it.

Generally, Qoheleth speaks of "portion" in a positive way, but he has a more negative view of **toil** (*'amal*), a term he uses to describe work, the fruits of one's labors, or even as a metaphor for life in general. Qoheleth is not opposed to the idea of work, and shows no patience for foolish or lazy people—he just can't forget that after all that work, someone else will inherit what he's earned, while he inherits a cold grave.

Despite his woeful moments, Qoheleth is not always pessimistic. He recognizes that there is **joy** (*simḥā*) to be found in life through eating, drinking, or enjoying the love of a spouse. On multiple occasions he advises people to live in the moment and take what joy they can in life (2:10, 24; 3:12, 22; 5:17-18; 8:15; 9:7-9; 11:7-10).

This may sound like a *carpe diem* philosophy. In the midst of his "royal fiction," when Qoheleth described himself as a rich king who experimented with every pleasure in his search for meaning, he said: "Whatever my eyes desired I did not keep from them; I kept my heart from no pleasure, for my heart found pleasure in all my toil, and this was my reward for all my toil" (2:10).

Along with his advice to enjoy life, Qoheleth acknowledges that experiencing such pleasure is the good gift of God, and not just an invitation to hedonism: "There is nothing better for mortals than to eat and drink, and find enjoyment in their toil," he said. "This also, I saw, is from the hand of God; for apart from him who can eat or who can have enjoyment?" (2:24-25).

Though he advises enjoyment, Qoheleth sees it as something of a concession: if people have to live this vain life under the sun, they might as well find some joy in it before they die. Thus, when he says "I know that there is nothing better for them than to be happy and enjoy themselves as long as they live" (3:12), the gist of his meaning is that, under the circumstances, it's the best they can do to find pleasure where they can, while remembering to be grateful: " … it is God's gift that all should eat and drink and take pleasure in all their toil" (3:13).

While endorsing enjoyment, Qoheleth never promotes excess or irresponsible behavior. He does not suggest that people should eat themselves sick, drink themselves drunk, or compromise morality just because it feels good.

This, Qoheleth believed, was the proper course of **wisdom** (*hokmā*), a favorite word of the sages and one that shows up no less than 52 times in Qoheleth. Wisdom is important to Qoheleth, though frustrating. He seeks to understand wisdom, but says he never found it (7:23-24). ♦ He writes within the basic purview of traditional wisdom, which holds that the fear of God, good sense, and good behavior lead to a successful life. But he is frustrated because it is obvious that the classic retribution theory doesn't always work, and he doesn't think it is

> 🔱 **Wisdom:** Qoheleth's claim that he searched for wisdom but never found it calls to mind a poem in Job 28 that also focuses on the elusiveness of wisdom. "But where shall wisdom be found?" Job asked, "And where is the place of understanding?" (v. 12).
>
> "Mortals do not know the way to it," Job concluded, "and it is not found in the land of the living" (v. 13). Wisdom could not be found in the depths of the sea or purchased for any amount of gold, silver, or jewels (vv. 14-19).
>
> Wisdom was hidden, Job thought, known only to God, who alone knew the secrets of the world and its weather (vv. 20-27). Thus, the best one could hope for was to receive this message from God: "And he said to humankind, 'Truly, the fear of the Lord, that is wisdom; and to depart from evil is understanding'" (v. 28).

fair. Wicked people may "prolong their life in evil-doing" (7:15) or be treated as righteous (8:14). Even fools might inherit riches, while their wise parents might have to leave them to him (2:18-19). 🔱

In Qoheleth's mind, "the same fate comes to the righteous and the wicked" (9:2): no wonder he considered it all vanity! Even though practical wisdom teachings may help a person get ahead in the world, have some success, and earn a portion of joy, he or she will still die at the end of it. The wise die just like fools, and there is not even a "portion" for those who are in the grave (9:6), nor will there be any lasting memory of the dead (2:16), as some hoped. Qoheleth believes that God is responsible for judgment (3:7, 8:5), but insists that understanding God's judgment is beyond human understanding.

While Qoheleth remains somewhat ambivalent about wisdom, there is no question about his opinion toward its antagonist: Qoheleth explicitly condemns folly (10:2-3) and never considers it a viable option. The old sage may have had

> 🔱 **Traditional wisdom:** The primary sources of traditional wisdom in the Bible are the book of Proverbs and the wisdom psalms, such as Pss. 1, 37, 49, 73, 112, 119, 127, 128, and 133. Psalm 1, for example, warns that wicked people who do not follow God's teachings will be like dry chaff that the wind blows away, while the wise who delight in God's law will be "like trees planted by streams of water, which yield their fruit in its season, and their leaves do not wither. In all that they do, they prosper" (Ps. 1:2-3).
>
> The book of Proverbs contains scores of injunctions promising success to those who fear God, obey the law, and work hard, while predicting only trials and trouble for those who are foolish, lazy, or apathetic toward God.

his questions about wisdom, but he sought it faithfully and had no dealings with fools. No less than traditional wisdom teachers, Qoheleth holds that one should **fear God** by standing in awe before God, remembering that God and humans are not in the same league (3:13, 5:6, 7:18, 8:12, 12:13). ♄

It has become evident that at the heart of Qoheleth's troubles is the knowledge that, sooner or later, no matter how righteous or wise or wealthy people are, they will die— and Qoheleth believed that death was the end. The writer of Proverbs found comfort in believing that the memory of the dead would live on (Prov. 10:7), but Qoheleth denied even that (1:11, 2:16).

As much as he hates the thought of death, Qoheleth suggests that in situations such as extreme suffering or oppression, death might be preferable to life. In 4:1, he speaks of people who are oppressed, with no one to deliver them or even to comfort them: "And I thought the dead, who have already died, more fortunate than the living, who are still alive; but better than both is the one who has not yet been, and has not seen the evil deeds that are done under the sun." (4:2-3). A similar thought, about one who is unable to find joy, is echoed in 6:1-6.

Outside of these circumstances, though, Qoheleth despises the thought of death. A poem about old age that closes the book (12:1-7)

♄ **Fear God:** The book of Qoheleth includes several references to the fear of God (3:14, 5:7, 7:18, 8:12), and concludes with the traditional advice to "fear God and keep his commandments, for that is the duty of everyone" (12:13). That last verse is found, however, in an epilogue (12:9-14) that was obviously written by someone who came after Qoheleth.

The writer of the epilogue praised Qoheleth's efforts and his "words of truth" (12:19), but cautioned against too much speculation: "The sayings of the wise are like goads, and like nails firmly fixed are the collected sayings given by one shepherd. Of anything beyond these, my child, beware" (12:11-12).

For the most part, Qoheleth seems to think of "fearing God" as keeping God and humankind in perspective, standing in awe before God even if God does seem inscrutable and unpredictable. To the fear of God, the author of the epilogue added "and keep his commandments," a subject Qoheleth had not addressed.

The epilogue also adds a warning about judgment. Qoheleth believed everyone died and shared the same fate, and did not think of God as particularly active in human affairs (7:14). He was not concerned about judgment, but the person behind the epilogue wanted to be sure that its readers conformed to traditional beliefs connecting human behavior and divine judgment.

describes a slow and painful march toward death, something he clearly does not anticipate with joy.

IS THERE ANY POINT?

So, what do we do with this biblical curmudgeon? Perhaps we should give a bit more attention to Qoheleth's belief that we should learn to do our best, but accept human limits and learn to appreciate the good things we have (2:10, 24; 3:12, 22; 5:17-18; 8:15; 9:7-9; 11:7-10).

The lengthiest version of Qoheleth's "best one can hope for" advice is an address to other men, the traditional targets of wisdom teachers:

> Go, eat your bread with enjoyment, and drink your wine with a merry heart; for God has long ago approved what you do. Let your garments always be white; do not let oil be lacking on your head. Enjoy life with the wife whom you love, all the days of your vain life that are given you under the sun, because that is your portion in life and in your toil at which you toil under the sun. Whatever your hand finds to do, do with your might; for there is no work or thought or knowledge or wisdom in Sheol, to which you are going. (9:7-10)

Qoheleth's advice is remarkably similar to a passage from the ancient Babylonian epic of Gilgamesh, who also struggled with the meaning of life. A large part of Gilgamesh's story is devoted to a quest for eternal life, but along the way a wise woman counseled him to enjoy the life he had rather than stressing over what he did not have (see "The Hardest Question" for more).

Qoheleth, as noted earlier, has no hope of life after death. Indeed, he goes so far as to imagine that humans and animals have the same fate:

> I said in my heart with regard to human beings that God is testing them to show that they are but animals. For the fate of humans and the fate of animals is the same; as one dies, so dies the other. They all have the same breath, and humans have no advantage over the animals; for all is vanity. All go to one place; all are from the dust, and all turn to dust again. Who knows whether the human spirit goes upward and the spirit of animals goes downward to the earth? (3:18-21)

Still, all was not lost. Even if humans are like animals, he concluded, they can be thankful that they live. Qoheleth may have been quoting an old proverb when he observed: "But whoever is joined with all the living has hope, for a living dog is better than a dead lion" (9:4).

Even that benefit is tainted, though: the one advantage the living have over the dead is that they can still think and know things—even if what they know is depressing: "The living know that they will die, but the dead know nothing; they have no more reward, and even the memory of them is lost" (9:5).

What, then, can we do with Qoheleth? The German scholar Hans W. Hertzberg reached a startling conclusion as he closed his commentary on Ecclesiastes by saying, "The book of Qoheleth, standing at the end of the Old Testament, is the most staggering messianic prophecy to appear in the Old Testament."[2]

How can this be? If nothing else, the book of Ecclesiastes reminds us of how frustrating or empty life can be without the hope of something beyond. The advice to enjoy the life we have is good for the moment, but it can only go so far. Qoheleth's compendium of bad news may be the best introduction we could have to the good news found in Jesus.

For Reflection: *What do you think about Hertzberg's comment regarding Qoheleth? How could such a humanistic and depressing book as Ecclesiastes be considered a messianic prophecy—especially a "staggering" one?*

THE HARDEST QUESTION
Was Qoheleth's advice original?

As noted in the lesson, Qoheleth was not the first to suggest that one should give up the quest of eternal life and learn to enjoy the life one has. The Gilgamesh Epic is known to us from clay tablets written in cuneiform, stretching over hundreds of years. The oldest fragments are in Sumerian, dating as far back as 2100 BCE. The Sumerian stories were collected and formed into a longer epic by the Babylonians probably between the 13th and 10th centuries, then copied many times over the following centuries. The best preserved version, containing about two-thirds of the original epic, is from an Assyrian collection of tablets from the ruins of Ashurbanipal's palace, dating to the 7th century BCE.

In the story, Gilgamesh was the great king of Uruk, born of a human father and a divine mother. This gave him extraordinary strength, size, and longevity—but no one to challenge him. In the epic, Gilgamesh became such a despot that the gods created a wild man named Enkidu to challenge him and stop him from oppressing his people. Gilgamesh and Enkidu confronted each other and fought, but in doing so became great friends and companions.

Gilgamesh and Enkidu engaged in a series of heroic adventures, including a journey to the Cedar Mountains, where they killed its guardian, a giant named Humbaba, so they could exploit the forest's rich resources. So heroic was Gilgamesh that the goddess Ishtar made romantic advances toward him, but he rebuffed her. Ishtar then sent the "Bull of Heaven" to punish Gilgamesh, but he and Enkidu killed it, prompting the gods to decree that Enkidu must die. Gilgamesh stayed by his friend as he grew weaker and died, even until his body decomposed to the point that a worm fell from his nose, convincing Gilgamesh that Enkidu would not awaken—and making him aware that he, too, could die.

Gilgamesh embarked on a quest to find eternal life, ultimately locating Utnapishtim, the hero of the Babylonian flood story, who told him of a plant that grew beneath the sea that could make one young again. Gilgamesh dove to the sea floor and obtained the plant, intending to take it home and test it on an old person before eating of it himself. On his way home, however, while Gilgamesh refreshed himself in a cool spring, a serpent ate the plant and slithered out of its skin, indicating that its youth had been restored (note the distant similarity to Genesis 3, where a serpent is also involved in the loss of eternal life for Adam and Eve).

Earlier, as Gilgamesh had made his way toward Utnapishtim's island, he had a conversation with a wise "alewife" (or "barmaid") who counseled Gilgamesh to give up on his quest for eternal life. The gods had decreed that humans' lot was to die, she said, and therefore Gilgamesh should give up on finding eternal life and learn to enjoy the life he had. Part of her advice, translated here from the Old Babylonian version, is so similar to Qoheleth's counsel that one has to assume the old sage was familiar with the story. Consider the two, side by side:

Gilgamesh (OB, Tablet X, iii. 6-14)	Qoheleth 9:7-9
You, Gilgamesh, let your belly be full—	Go, eat your bread with joyfulness,
Day and night have joy in yourself— Every day establish joy, every night dance and play.	And drink your wine with a happy heart (for God is already pleased with your actions)
Let your garments be clean— Your head, let it be washed, Bathe yourself in water.	At all times let your garments be white, And oil on your head, Let it not be lacking.
Look upon the little child who holds your hand, (Your) spouse, let her rejoice in your lap,	Experience life with the woman you love...
This is the task of (humankind).	...for it is your portion in life.

NOTES

[1]Roland Murphy, *Ecclesiastes*, vol. 23A, Word Biblical Commentary (Zondervan, 1992), lviii-lxix.

[2]Hans W. Hertzberg, *Der Prediger* (KAT XVII/4, 1963), 238.

ESTHER

A New Hope

A TALE OF TWO HEROINES

The king loved Esther more than all the other women;
of all the virgins she won his favor and devotion,
so that he set the royal crown on her head and made her queen instead of Vashti.
—Esther 2:17

D o you have any heroes? Heroes don't have to be famous: they can be people who have impressed you with their courage, their hard work, their care for others, or some other especially admirable quality.

When I was in high school I considered my football coach, Thomas Bunch, to be a hero. I admired his combination of leadership and real concern for each player. In college I looked up to Bryan Edwards, who directed the Baptist Student Union at the University of Georgia. Later I came to consider Fred Rogers, of *Mr. Rogers' Neighborhood*, as a hero of compassion and an advocate for children.

Your heroes may or may not be people who are well known. Sometimes the most unlikely people can do heroic things, even if they are unsung and unrewarded for it. The initial chapters of Esther contain the stories of two women who did heroic things, though one of them was exiled for her actions. Esther became famous as a savior of Israel, but her story acknowledges that she would not have been in a place to do so if not for the integrity of another heroic woman.

A COURAGE-DRIVEN FALL
(1:1-21)

Our study of the Megillot has shown that women play featured roles. The Song of Songs would be just half of a song if not for the beloved woman's role: it takes two. The book of Ruth includes a few male characters, but is clearly centered on the bereaved Naomi and her daughter-in-law, Ruth. When the author of Lamentations mourned the destruction of Jerusalem, he personified the city as a woman, "Daughter Zion." Ecclesiastes was written by a man whose audience would have been men, but he counseled them to appreciate and enjoy the love of their wives. Now we come to Esther, another story in which the lead character is a woman. While Ruth lived as a foreigner among Hebrews, Esther was a Jew living among foreigners.

The short book of Esther appears in the Hebrew Bible as one of five books called the Megillot, or "Scrolls," each of which was read in conjunction with a major Jewish feast. Esther is read today during the Feast of Purim, which honors her heroism.

The story is set in Persia under a king most English translations call Ahaseurus, an unknown king name that some scholars identify with Xerxes I (486–465 BCE), and others with Artaxerxes I (465–424 BCE). The king is said to have ruled over lands from Egypt to Afghanistan, similar in size to what we know of the ancient Persian Empire (1:1). 👆

With this king, everything is supersized. The story claims that he threw a banquet for his nobles that lasted for 180 days. Can you imagine a feast that goes on for six months? Afterward, the story says he presided over a seven-day banquet for ordinary men, while Queen Vashti hosted a weeklong banquet for women (1:2-9). 👆

👆 King who? The Hebrew spelling of the king's name is *Ahashverosh*, usually rendered in English as Ahaseurus (the Hebrew letter rendered "v" in Ahashverosh could also be taken as a "u," and the letters for "s" and "sh" were originally the same, so the transliteration is uncertain). This does not match any of the Persian king names we know from other records. Both Xerxes I (486–465) and Artaxerexes I (465–424) have been suggested as alternate names for the king. The Septuagint translated it as Artaxerxes. At least one modern translation, the NIV, renders it as Xerxes.

According to Persian records, Xerxes' queen was named Amestris: there is no mention of either Vashti or Esther (nor do the Persian records show other kings who had wives by those names). Other details in the book are highly at odds with what is known about Persia during that period, and the king is described in cartoonish rather than regal fashion. This leads many readers to wonder if the book should be considered historical, or whether it was a fictional account given a historical setting, designed to encourage the Jews during a difficult time. Critical scholars tend to prefer the second option.

> **U Society news:** The account of King Ahaseurus' banquet, which was reportedly for every person in Susa but also small enough to fit in the palace courtyard, could have been written by a society columnist:
>
> There were white cotton curtains and blue hangings tied with cords of fine linen and purple to silver rings and marble pillars. There were couches of gold and silver on a mosaic pavement of porphyry, marble, mother-of-pearl, and colored stones. Drinks were served in golden goblets, goblets of different kinds, and the royal wine was lavished according to the bounty of the king. Drinking was by flagons, without restraint; for the king had given orders to all the officials of his palace to do as each one desired. (Est. 1:6-8)

On the seventh day of the banquet, the story says, when the king was under the influence of too much wine, he sent seven royal officials who attended him to bring Queen Vashti so he could show her off to the drunken revelers. U He wanted her to come, the text says, "wearing the royal crown, in order to show the peoples and the officials her beauty, for she was fair to behold" (1:10-11).

Was the crown all that he expected her to wear, or did he want her to dance for the crowd? Whatever he expected would have involved putting herself on display before a courtyard filled with drunken party-goers, and Vashti did not wish to cheapen herself in such a tawdry environment, so she refused to come. The embarrassed king was enraged, as we might imagine.

What can a king do with a non-submissive wife? By demanding her presence—apparently in a loud-enough voice for the crowd to hear—the king had foolishly pushed himself into a corner. Needing to save face, he called on his counselors, who insisted that a decisive response was needed. Vashti's failure to obey had not only wronged the king, they argued, but also set a dangerous precedent that could impact every man in the kingdom. Other women might assume that if Queen Vashti could disobey the king, they could follow suit and disobey their husbands (1:13-17). Indeed, the officials said: "This very day the noble ladies of

> **U Triple sevens:** Note the sequence of sevens: on the seventh day of the party, the sotted king sent seven eunuchs to fetch Queen Vashti, and then consulted seven court officials when she refused. The number seven typically symbolizes wholeness—as in the seven days of creation. For the hapless king, however, the lengthy party dissolves into chaos.

Persia and Media who have heard of the queen's behavior will rebel against the king's officials, and there will be no end of contempt and wrath!" (1:18).

To minimize the damage, the senior advisors called for drastic action, recommending that Queen Vashti should be banished, and a new queen chosen "who is better than she" (1:19). Notice of the banishment should be put into an irrevocable decree and proclaimed throughout the Persians' vast empire, they said, so that "all women will give honor to their husbands, high and low alike" so that "every man should be master in his own house" (1:20-22). ♦

The narrator's portrayal of the officials' insecurity and fear that Vashti's actions could destabilize Persian society seems almost cartoonish, but most characters in the story are portrayed in over-the-top fashion. The author shows no special sympathy for Vashti, but appears to harbor a certain respect for her integrity. It was essential to the plot that the former queen be dispatched so Esther could rise to take her place, but the author is careful to attribute her banishment to the Persian king's drunken and foolish demand and his senior staff's panicked response. While Vashti's role in the story serves mainly to make way for Esther and to foreshadow the danger of offending the king, her strength of character and willingness to disobey her drunken husband stand as heroic virtues that should not be lost in Esther's shadow.

> ♦ **Neither snow nor sleet:** The reference to sending a proclamation in the form of letters in various languages throughout the Persian Empire (1:21-22), along with other references in the book, reflect one reality that we know of: ancient Persia was known to have an elaborate postal system.

For Reflection: *American society in general is far less patriarchal than the social context portrayed through most of the Old Testament, but many people still believe—arguing from the Bible—that women should be subordinate to men, especially in marriage. Do you believe wives should play a more submissive role based on their gender?*

A STEALTHY WOMAN'S RISE
(2:1–23)

With the banishment of Vashti, the king was left without a trophy wife, though we presume he still had access to a harem of available women. When he had sobered up and his anger had subsided, he seems to have regretted his actions as "he remembered Vashti and what she had done and what had been decreed against her" (2:1). To fill the void, his advisers sought to cheer him up by suggesting an empire-wide search for a new queen. The king should appoint commissioners in every province, they said, to choose the most beautiful young virgins and send them to the palace as potential brides. "Let the girl who pleases the king be queen instead of Vashti," they said, and Ahaseurus liked the idea (2:2-4).

The process was quite elaborate: the young women were to be brought to the palace and housed in the king's harem, where they would undergo an extensive process of purification and beauty treatments, in addition to training in courtly manners and feminine arts. Then, one by one, they were brought to the king for an overnight visit so he could choose among them (2:12-14). 🙿

One of the promising candidates was Esther, a young Hebrew woman who had been raised by her older cousin Mordecai after her parents had died. Mordecai's great-grandfather Kish had been among the citizens of Jerusalem that Nebuchadnezzar had forced into Babylonian exile (2:5-6). His family had remained there rather than returning to Jerusalem and apparently settled in Susa, a city used by the Persian kings as their winter capital (now in western Iran).

🙿 **Persian idol:** The king's talent search was quite elaborate. Prospective candidates were brought into a preparatory harem presided over by a man named Hegai, described as a eunuch (it was common in the ancient world for officials with access to royal women to be castrated). In Hegai's training harem, the women spent a full year having beauty treatments: "six months with oil of myrrh and six months with perfumes and cosmetics for women" (2:12). When each woman's turn came for a night with the king, she would go to him in the evening, taking whatever clothing or supplies she wished. On the morning after, she would proceed to a second harem supervised by Shaashgaz, another eunuch. There she would remain unless the king called for her again (2:13-14).

Esther was the daughter of Mordecai's uncle, but evidently much younger than him. Her parents must have died when she was quite young, for the text says that Mordecai adopted Esther and raised her as his own daughter (2:7). Esther's

Hebrew name was Hadassah (which means "Myrtle"), but at some point she became known as Esther, a Persian word meaning "Star," similar to the Babylonian Ishtar, a goddess whose icon was a star.

From the beginning, the narrator portrays Esther as living up to her star billing. We learn from v. 7 that she "had a beautiful figure and was pleasant to look at" (a rather literal translation). As a result, she was among those who were chosen to train and compete for the king's affections.

After arriving in the harem designed for virgins, Esther soon charmed Hegai, the eunuch who oversaw the training program, so that "he quickly provided her with her cosmetic treatments and her portion of food, and with seven chosen maids from the king's palace, and advanced her and her maids to the best place in the harem" (2:8). Esther's popularity was such that she "was admired by all who saw her" (2:15), presumably including the other young women.

Despite being in the harem spotlight, Esther had a secret: following the advice of Mordecai, Esther used only her Persian name and did not tell anyone that she was a Jew (2:10-11, 20). The reader may find it surprising that her ethnicity could have remained secret, for every day her guardian Mordecai, who also served in the palace, "would walk around in front of the court of the harem" to see how Esther was doing, and Mordecai was known to be a Jew.

Esther's beauty, charm, and talents made an equal impression on the king, for when her turn came to spend the night with him, "the king loved Esther more than all the other women; of all the virgins she won his favor and devotion, so that he set the royal crown on her head and made her queen instead of Vashti" (2:17). Esther must have been singularly pleasing. Not only did she rise above the other young women, but also made the king so happy that he held a court dinner in her honor for all of his officials and ministers, declared a holiday throughout the empire, and "gave gifts with royal liberality" (2:18).

The act of heroism for which Esther would be forever remembered has yet to occur, but the narrator has already portrayed her as a credit to her people, a Jew (though secretly) who outshone the most beautiful young women of the kingdom to win the king's heart. The narrator is unperturbed by the implicit immorality involved in her ascent: after a year of beauty treatments and courtly training in the harem for virgins, the women were brought to the king in the evening and escorted to a different harem the next morning. We may safely assume that their purpose was not solely to sit for an interview or engage the king in witty conversation. Though the queen-selection derby was not of her own making, Esther chose to make the best of her circumstances. That she slept her way to the throne did not bother the narrator, who apparently saw her ascent as providential (4:12-14).

Esther is not the only Old Testament woman to be honored despite actions contrary to traditional expectations. Tamar pretended to be a prostitute in order to get pregnant by her father-in-law after Judah refused to let his youngest son marry her when his brothers died, as custom demanded (Genesis 38). Rahab was known as a harlot, but praised for her actions in hiding Israelite spies (Josh. 6:25, Heb. 11:31, Jas. 2:25). Ruth won Boaz's heart after following Naomi's advice to get dolled up and crawl under the blankets with him (Ruth 3:1-13). Abigail went behind her husband's back to supply David with provisions, and when Nabal died shortly thereafter, she quickly married David (1 Samuel 25). They were not alone.

The Old Testament often recognizes the valor of women who did what they had to do to survive, even when they had to venture outside the box of normally acceptable behavior. Heroes come in many forms.

For Reflection*: Can you think of situations in your life that might call for unconventional action?*

THE HARDEST QUESTION
How did the book of Esther get into the Bible?

It is difficult, from a literary perspective, to classify the book of Esther. It is often called a novella, although scenes are not fully developed and the whole does not flow together well. In general, the narrative follows the typical pattern of a good story. It begins by introducing the main characters (1:1–2:23), who then face a series of dramatic complications resulting in a crisis (3:1–8:17) that finally reaches a resolution (9:1–10:3).

The book of Esther exists in two forms that are quite different. The standard Hebrew version of the text is reflected in Protestant Bibles. It contains 10 chapters, none of which make any reference to God, to prayer, or to a covenant with Israel. At some point this was recognized as problematic, and a later author added six additional sections of text, including several prayers that carefully include the name of God. This material is included in the version of Esther found in the Septuagint, the early Greek translation of the Old Testament. As such, it is also considered to be scripture in Catholic Bibles. Protestant Bibles that contain the Apocrypha include these sections as "Additions to Esther."

The sharp variation in the two early versions suggests that the story has troubled readers since shortly after its composition, and for good reason. The Hebrew version (called the Masoretic text, or MT) is almost certainly the most original, and is considerably shorter than the Greek version. The book's failure to mention the name of God even once, or to attribute the deliverance to God, is one of the reasons it was controversial. Not everyone wanted it in the canon. Its value was disputed for centuries after the Hebrew canon closed. Later, Martin Luther reportedly wrote in one of his "Table Talks" that he wished Esther had never found its way into the canon, believing it displayed too much heathen influence and gave the Jews undue prominence.

The Greek version seeks to fill in perceived blanks in the Hebrew text by adding six additional passages. These give more attention to Mordecai, and are laced with portents, visions, and prophesies. The additions also include several prayers of Mordecai and Esther, which serve to insert God's name seven times. In the Greek version, primary emphasis also shifts from the deliverance of the Jews to God's favor being shown to Esther and Mordecai.

How are we to understand the book's purpose? The author seems to be interested in several things. Early on, the rabbis considered Esther as a retelling of the Exodus story, and we can see why. As in the Exodus story, a Jew is inserted into a foreign court, where a royal official attempts to kill the Jews, but a reversal of fortunes results in their salvation.

Conservative writers tend to date the book of Esther to the Persian period, when it purportedly took place, while others think it more likely to have been written three centuries later, when the people were in extreme duress under Antiochus Epiphanes IV, and they needed encouragement such as that provided by the heroic Esther, who risked her life to save her people.

Some commentators have noted a similarity of names between characters in the book and certain Babylonian and Persian gods, for example: The names Esther and Mordecai are Hebrew equivalents to the leading Babylonian gods Ishtar and Marduk. Vashti's name is similar to that of a Persian goddess named Mashti. The villain Haman's name recalls a Persian god called Hamman.

Thus, some scholars suspect there may have been a popular Babylonian tale reflecting a struggle between the Babylonian and Persian gods that was adapted to and romanticized for a Jewish audience. The names Mordecai and Esther mean nothing in Hebrew, but are good Akkadian names (both the Babylonian and Assyrian languages were dialects of Akkadian). Likewise, the word "*pur*" in "Purim," referring to lots cast to determine the day on which the Jews would be killed, is also an Akkadian word.

Whenever the book was written, Esther remains a clear reminder of the many dangers the Jewish people have faced through the years. Like the Persians described in Esther, majority populations in various countries have often made diaspora Jews their scapegoats, accusing them of various outrageous and unfounded evils, such as killing children or poisoning water supplies. As recent as 80 years ago, Hitler and his Fascists sought to exterminate every Jew they could reach, and succeeded in murdering six million Jewish people (plus five million others considered to be undesirable). It's no wonder that the book of Esther is so cherished by the Jews and celebrated each year during the Feast of Purim.

Esther 7:1-6, 9-10; 9:20-22

A WINNING WOMAN

Then Queen Esther answered,
"If I have won your favor, O king, and if it pleases the king,
let my life be given me—that is my petition—
and the lives of my people—that is my request."
—Esther 7:3

J ealousy. Have you ever felt it? Have you ever said something spiteful or even done something hurtful out of envy toward someone else? Have you been on the other side of the equation, when someone sought to defame or harm you because they were jealous?

The book of Esther tells the story of a brave woman's heroic actions to save her people—people who needed saving, in large part, because of jealousy. A powerful man's dangerous combination of racist attitudes and jealous anger endangered every Jew in Persia. How did it start?

ESTHER'S PREDICAMENT

The story of Esther's unexpected ascension to become queen of Persia (1:1–2:18) is followed by a brief account of political intrigue that sets the stage for conflict to come. First, we learn that Esther's guardian Mordecai had some position that allowed him access to the palace grounds. Ancient Susa consisted of a lower city for common people and a fortified acropolis where the palace and administrative quarters were located. Shortly after Esther's wedding banquet he was reportedly "sitting at the king's gate," where royal business was transacted, when he learned that two of the guards had become angry with the king and were plotting to assassinate him. Mordecai told Esther about the threat, who reported it to Ahasuerus in Mordecai's name. The would-be assassins were hanged (or possibly impaled) and the affair was recorded in the annals of the king, a record that would play a role later in the story (2:21-23).

Next, we are introduced to a high official named Haman, who gained sufficient favor with the king to be promoted to a seat "above all the officials who were with him." ♆ This apparently entitled him to a display of respect from lower officials who served at the gate, who "bowed down and did obeisance to Haman"—with the notable exception of Mordecai, who refused to kneel (3:1-2). Moredecai's refusal to bow, which per-

> ♆ **Haman's ancestry:** While Mordecai was identified as a Benjaminite, Haman is described as an "Agagite," which the rabbis interpreted to mean that he was descended of the Amalekites, among Israel's fiercest enemies. A king of Amalek, defeated by Saul and killed by Samuel, was named Agag (1 Samuel 15). Haman, then, is not just a jealous court official, but a representative of Israel's oldest enemy: he is anti-Semitism personified.

sisted day after day, appears to be related to his religion. Though other officials tried to persuade him not to provoke Haman, Mordecai still refused to bow, "for he had told them that he was a Jew" (3:4). Israel's law did not prohibit bowing before kings or high officials, but Mordecai may have believed he should bow only before God. ♆

Mordecai's refusal to bow infuriated Haman, who assumed that he had the authority to order Mordecai's death, but he wasn't satisfied with that: his resentment of the Jews was so deep that he set in motion a plot to exterminate every Jew in the Persian Empire (3:5-6). Haman persuaded the king that all members of "a certain people" scattered throughout the land were disloyal, followed their own laws, and should be exterminated. He had chosen the 13th of Adar as a propitious date for the genocide by casting lots (*purim*), and promised to deliver at least 10,000 talents of silver to the royal treasury, to be acquired by plundering the offensive but unnamed ethnic group. The king, apparently without asking who

> ♆ **Mordecai's motivation:** The traditional Hebrew text does not explain Mordecai's reasoning for not bowing to Haman. The Greek additions, however, include a prayer in which Mordecai said he did not refuse out of pride or personal glory, but "I did this so that I might not set human glory above the glory of God, and I will not bow down to anyone but you, who are my Lord; and I will not do these things in pride" (Addition C: 13:12-14).

the "certain people" were, gave Haman authority to wipe them out and turned over his signet ring so that Haman could send out public proclamations with the seal of the king (3:7-12). ⛏

The royal letters gave "orders to destroy, to kill, and to annihilate all Jews, young and old, women and children in one day, the thirteenth day of the twelfth month, which is the month of Adar, and to plunder their goods" (3:13). While conniving Haman and the witless king sat down to drink, "the city of Susa was thrown into confusion" (3:14-15). Why the king remained oblivious to the identity of Haman's target group, and why he did not recognize the depth of the atrocity, is unstated.

> ⛏ **A political cartoon?** Kandy Queen-Sutherland has noted that the book of Esther "has a political cartoon quality about it, where the reader at times may chuckle, at other times gasp, and in the end recognize truth."
>
> The king, for example, is portrayed in exaggerated fashion: he is powerful and skillful enough to rule an empire, yet foolish enough to make drunken demands of his wife and to authorize the extermination of a people without even asking who they were.[1]

Mordecai soon learned of the plot, of course, and went into public mourning, wearing sackcloth and "wailing with a loud cry" throughout the city. Jews throughout the kingdom joined the obvious display of mourning, but the king apparently remained unaware or paid it no heed (4:1-3). Esther was also distressed, and sent a messenger to Mordecai requesting more information about the plot, which Mordecai provided in detail—along with a plea that she intercede with the king about the planned pogrom (4:4-8).

Esther, whose Jewish identity had remained secret, recited a rule that anyone who approached the king "inside the inner court" without being called was subject to death if the king did not show immediate favor—then noted that 30 days had passed since he last called for her (4:9-11).

Mordecai reminded Esther that if the genocide was allowed to go on, she would be killed anyway, for her identity would certainly become known. Mordecai further suggested that there was a deeper plan behind Esther's phenomenal rise: If she would not speak up, then help might come "from another quarter," the closest thing to a mention of God in the Hebrew version of the book. But perhaps, Mordecai said, Esther had been brought to royalty "for such a time as this," to be in position to save her people (4:12-14).

After fasting for three days, during which she asked all other Jews to fast (4:15-17), Esther gathered her courage and approached the king, who not only accepted her, but also promised to grant any boon she wanted—up to half the kingdom (5:1-3).

> ⛊ **Tension:** The reader might wonder what Esther's purpose was in having
> the dinner, but still holding off on revealing her plan and inviting the king and
> Haman to a second dinner on the next day. Whatever Esther might have had in
> mind, the narrator uses the episode to build tension by having the reader wait
> for a resolution.

Why did Esther not ask immediately that the edict be cancelled, or at least amended to blunt its effects? Ahaseurus had offered up to half of the kingdom! Apparently she had a more dramatic resolution in mind, and one that makes for a better story. Having been granted a boon, Esther asked only that the king and Haman come to a dinner that she would prepare (5:4). At the dinner, the narrator tells us, the king renewed his offer, but again Esther delayed, requesting that the two men return for another meal the next day (5:5-8). ⛊

> **For Reflection:** *Imagine that you somehow found yourself in a setting where either governmental authorities or local vigilantes had announced a plan to locate and execute all Christian believers. What would you do?*

ESTHER'S PLAN
(7:1-6, 9-10; 9:20-22)

The plot now moves quickly. Haman was so elated by the honor of being singled out for dinner with the royal couple that he was fit to burst, but when Mordecai again refused to bow, he became furious. After arriving at home, Haman complained to his wife and friends that his honors and wealth meant nothing when Mordecai wouldn't bow to him. They suggested that a public hanging for Mordecai might make him feel better, and Haman quickly ordered that a ridiculously high 75-foot gallows (or possibly a stake for impalement) be erected for his nemesis' execution (5:9-14).

Meanwhile, back at the palace, the king had insomnia, and called for someone to read court records to him. When the records reminded him of how Mordecai had saved his life, the king realized that he had failed to reward Mordecai (6:1-3).

A large dose of Hebrew humor enters the story when Haman just happened to be found standing in the court, probably intending to gain the king's endorsement of his plan to execute Mordecai. Before he could make a request, the king asked him for advice on how to honor a royal favorite. Assuming that he himself would be the honoree, the proud Haman proposed that the king's robes and crown should be put on the man, he should be seated on the king's horse, and one of the king's highest officials should lead him through the streets shouting "Thus it shall be done for he who pleases the king!" (6:4-9).

To his chagrin, Haman was then instructed to go out and do that very thing for the despised Mordecai, leading Mordecai's horse in a walk of shame that would have delighted Hebrew readers. He returned home feeling disgraced, where his wife and friends berated him before he was summoned to the second dinner with Esther (6:10-14).

Finally, the moment of truth arrived. As the king repeated his offer to give her up to half the kingdom (7:2), Esther asked for something more important than material things: she asked for her life, and the lives of her people (7:3).

The story assumes the king would have been puzzled by this. Unaware that Esther was a Jew, he had not known that her life was in jeopardy. Borrowing language from Haman's proclamation that the king had authorized, she continued: "For we have been sold, I and my people, to be destroyed, to be killed, and to be annihilated." ♦ If the Jews had only been sold into slavery, Esther insisted, she might have held her peace, but if the genocide was carried out, she said,

---

♦ **Destroyed, killed, and annihilated:** Note the rhetorical power of Esther's statement as she makes the king aware of Haman's plot. "For we have been sold, I and my people, to be destroyed, to be killed, and to be annihilated" (7:4; cf. 3:13).

Esther first emphasized that *she*, along with her people, had been "sold"—the king had not been aware that Esther was Jewish, but still he had signed an order allowing Haman to have all the Jews killed, while plundering them for resources to pay 10,000 talents of silver into the treasury.

The three verbs indicating the end result of Haman's plot are all infinitives, and could be translated as "to destruction and to slaughter and to annihilation" (so NET). Esther wanted the king to know that he had authorized a full-fledged genocide—one that would include his queen.

When the king allowed Mordecai to pen a decree counteracting Haman's earlier order for the Jews to be killed, Mordecai repeated the language:

> By these letters the king allowed the Jews who were in every city to assemble and defend their lives, to destroy, to kill, and to annihilate any armed force of any people or province that might attack them, with their children and women, and to plunder their goods on a single day throughout all the provinces of King Ahasuerus, on the thirteenth day of the twelfth month, which is the month of Adar. (8:11-12)

Damage to the king? The translation of the last part of 7:4 is difficult, because some of the words could have multiple meanings. Thus, it could be "no enemy can compensate for this damage to the king" (NRSV), or "no such distress could justify disturbing the king" (NIV, similar translations in NET, HCSB).

If the former translation is correct, the queen seems to be suggesting that the king's reputation would have been damaged beyond repair, or perhaps that the nation's economy would be harmed if he had committed genocide against the Jews.

If the second translation is correct, Esther's point is that the king is so mighty that enslaving the Jews (including her) would have been beneath his notice, and that she only troubled him with the matter because it would cause the extermination of an entire people (again, including her).

The overall setting makes the latter option more likely: the king is portrayed as being extraordinarily powerful and unwilling to be troubled by minor matters. By explaining the danger to her people in such humble fashion, Esther strategically wins the favor of the king.

"no enemy can compensate for this damage to the king" (7:4).

When Esther then fingered Haman as the wicked "foe and enemy" (7:5-6), the king went into a rage and left the room. Quailing in fear, Haman fell upon Esther to beg for mercy, but when the king returned and saw Haman fawning at Esther's knees, he accused him of trying to assault the queen and grew so incensed that he ordered his servants to hang Haman on the very gallows he had constructed for Mordecai (7:7-10). He then gave Haman's house to Esther and elevated Mordecai to Haman's former position, giving him the royal signet ring he had taken back from Haman (8:1-2).

Though the reader may feel relieved, the story is not over nor the danger ended, for the plot requires that the edict ordering that the Jews be killed on the 13th of Adar could not be changed. At Esther's urging, however, the king allowed Esther and Mordecai to fashion a second royal edict allowing the Jews to defend themselves and "to annihilate any armed force of any people or province that might attack them with their children and women, and

The law of the Medes and the Persians: Both the book of Daniel (6:8, 12, 15) and Esther (1:19) speak of "the law of the Medes and the Persians," which cannot be changed, and the irrevocability of the law plays an important role in the plot of the story. Extrabiblical confirmation of the law, from known Persian or other historical sources, is lacking.

to plunder them" on the desig-
nated day (8:3-12).

The news brought such relief
to the Jews that " the city of Susa
shouted and rejoiced," and "for the
Jews there was light and gladness,
joy and honor." They called for a
holiday to celebrate, and many
who had remained secret Jews
came out of the closet and openly
expressed their Hebrew identity
(8:13-17). ♻

With the better part of a year
to prepare, the Hebrews organized
their defense, and when the day

> ♻ **Mordecai's robes:** The author's
> delight in social detail, evidenced in
> the description of the king's banquet
> in 1:5-8, returns with his account of
> Mordecai's triumphant parade through
> Susa after having persuaded the king to
> grant the Jews relief. "Then Mordecai
> went out from the presence of the king,
> wearing royal robes of blue and white,
> with a great golden crown and a mantle
> of fine linen and purple, while the city
> of Susa shouted and rejoiced" (8:15).

arrived, according to the story, the Jews became the aggressors, reportedly killing
75,000 persons in the provinces and another 800 in the capital, where Esther
persuaded the king to allow the rampage to continue for a second day (9:1-16).

So, the story says, the Jews in the countryside won relief on the 13th of Adar
and celebrated on the 14th, while Jews in Susa took their vengeance on the 13th
and 14th, not stopping to feast and celebrate until the 15th. It is for this reason, the
text says, that Mordecai issued an edict declaring that the Feast of Purim should
be celebrated on both the 14th and 15th of the month of Adar (9:20-22). The story
is clearly idealized: nearly 75,800 enemies reportedly died while no Jews were
killed, and the next day was devoted to a party. What kind of war was that?

For Reflection: *To this day, Jews around the world celebrate the Feast of
Purim on the 14th of Adar, in a few places continuing through the 15th. The
celebration typically includes a meal, an exchange of gifts, donations to charity, special prayers, and a reading of the book of Esther. Do any Christian
observances remind you of this?*

ESTHER'S AFTERMATH

Such a story. It's quite entertaining, but can Christian believers find anything
helpful in the book of Esther? It's not easy.

One could argue, perhaps, that one reading of the book promotes balanced
living, as opposed to the excesses of the king and his court, or that it testifies to
the power of the written word, with emphasis on the various edicts issued.

🔸 **Esther and Hitler:** During World War II, European Jews gave special attention to Esther, which recounted another time in which Jews faced hostility and persecution led by a zealous opponent. In reading the book during Purim, even when in secret, they thought of Hitler as Haman. For his part, Hitler was familiar with the book of Esther. He spoke against the celebration of Purim in one of his radio speeches castigating the Jews as a danger to Europe. He also confiscated scrolls of Esther, burning them and banning the observance of Purim.[2]

For greater profit, we have to imagine ourselves in the place of the Jewish people for whom the book was written. While we have little interest in the rationale for dating the Feast of Purim, other aspects of the story may be more meaningful.

The Jewish people, who have continued to be persecuted through the years, found in Esther a continued promise of hope for difficult times. 🔸 Although there is no direct correlation to the kind of threat faced by Esther and her people, we know that we all face difficult and trying days. In that generic sense, readers may find encouragement in Esther's perseverance through troubled times.

We may also find inspiration in Esther's careful planning. The story portrays her as living in a delicate balance, having to walk a fine line in dealing with the king. In that sense, Esther's ability to develop a plan and finesse its success may speak to our own need for giving careful thought to our various activities and our relationships with others.

Additionally, we may take heart in Esther's courage. Convinced by Mordecai that she had the ability to save her people, Esther was willing to do what needed to be done, even at considerable risk. If we don't recognize the risks inherent in truly following Jesus, perhaps we haven't been following closely enough.

For Reflection: *When you consider the story of Esther, what lessons or encouragement do you find there? Would you hold up Esther and Mordecai as role models for your children?*

THE HARDEST QUESTION
What about Esther's dark side?

Readers may be troubled by some indications that the sweet and virginal Esther had a dark side. On the one hand, she gained her position as queen by sleeping with the king. Whether she could have refused the assignment without dire consequences is unknown, but she must have approached it with some enthusiasm, given that the king was so taken with her beauty and bedroom charm that he chose her as queen. Even so, the text offers no criticism for Esther, but congratulates her. Esther did what she needed to do, and happily found herself in a position to aid all the Jews.

On the other hand, once she gained a position of power and influence with the king, Esther revealed a surprisingly vengeful side. When the appointed day of attack and defense arrived, the Persians appear to have held back while the Jews became aggressors, reportedly killing 75,000 of their "enemies" throughout the provinces (the text uses the same words for "slaughter" and "destroy" that Esther had used in telling the king that the Jews were threatened with slaughter and destruction, 7:4, 9:5).

At the end of the day, the king asked what she thought about the Jews' killing of 500 Persians in the capital city of Susa, including Haman's 10 sons. Esther, surprisingly, showed a bloodthirsty streak. She asked that the sons' bodies be hanged on public display, and that the Jews be allowed to continue their vengeance for a second day—when another 300 were reportedly killed.

Some interpreters argue that the book was not intended to celebrate the extended massacre, but to focus on deliverance only. Still, one cannot ignore the narrator's apparent delight in tallying the dead, though he points out that the Jews "did not touch the plunder" (9:10, 15-16) to emphasize that they were only interested in deliverance, not material gain.

Careful readers may find this turn of events surprising, if not shocking. It may be helpful, then, to consider the setting. The book was probably written at a time when the Jews were severely outnumbered and under intense persecution. Emphasis on the radical turn of fortune for the Jews in Esther's story could have encouraged the bedraggled Jews of a later day to persevere and to believe that they might also win an unexpected victory.

While Jews who faced persecution have often taken solace in the book of Esther, others have taken it further. Some radical Jewish interpreters, notably Meir Kahane, founder of the Jewish Defense League, have employed Esther to develop a theology of revenge. Kahane argued that the establishment of the modern State of Israel should be seen as a divine act of revenge in response to the constant persecution of Jews, and obligated Jews to take revenge against all who opposed them.[3]

How should Christian readers view the issue of revenge in Esther? When we look at Esther through the lens of the New Testament, we recall Jesus' teaching that we should not hate our enemies or take vengeance on them, but love them and pray for them (Matt. 5:44; Luke 6:27, 35). War and killing may sometimes seem to be necessary evils, but vengeful and unnecessary slaughter is clearly beyond acceptable behavior for believers.

NOTES

[1]Kandy Queen-Southerland, "Esther," in *Mercer Commentary on the Bible* (Mercer University Press, 1995), 395-97.

[2]For more, see Kandy Queen-Sutherland, *Ruth and Esther*, Smyth & Helwys Commentary (Smyth & Helwys, 2016), 205-207.

[3]For more, see Queen-Sutherland, 208-210.

AFTERWORD

In studying the Megillot, we are taken on a journey through much of Israel's history, at least in metaphorical fashion. The Song of Songs, though patently about the love of a man and a woman, has been allegorized through the years to represent God's love for Israel, especially during the early years of their covenant relationship, which the prophets later thought of as a "honeymoon" period.

The book of Ruth, with its tale of how Naomi found redemption and how Obed was born, foreshadows not only the birth of Obed's grandson David, but also the birth of the monarchy and the onset of Israel's "glory days."

Hebrew hegemony was short lived, however. The united kingdom lasted less than 100 years before splitting into two parts. Both Israel and Judah were conquered, their cities destroyed, and their people scattered or taken into exile.

The book of Lamentations bemoans Judah's loss and Jerusalem's burning in specific and touching ways. The book of Ecclesiastes never references the exile, but questions Israel's theology as well as its wisdom, coming up empty.

When hope had grown rare and even the Jews living in Persia were threatened, Esther arose to deliver her people and engender new hope for the Jews, inspiring a culture of perseverance and loyalty to Judaism that persists to this day.

When Christians read the Megillot, we are reminded that the roots of our faith extend deep into the Old Testament, and encompass these same stories of testimony and tenaciousness.

We too may celebrate the relationship of love we can have with God (and with our spouses). We too may find comfort in the memory of strong and happy days of personal faith and a healthy church.

But, we may also have experienced personal sorrow leading to a crisis of faith, and find comfort in knowing we are not the first or the last. Ultimately, we too may find hope—not through the shedding of our enemies' blood, but through Christ's unselfish life on earth and death on the cross.

Whether Hebrew or Christian, our faith may have ups and downs, but God's last word is always one of hope.

www.ingramcontent.com/pod-product-compliance
Lightning Source LLC
Chambersburg PA
CBHW062115080426
42734CB00012B/2878